For Heath...

$19⁹⁵

BUSINESS MENSCH

TIMELESS WISDOM
FOR TODAY'S ENTREPRENEUR

Best Wishes!

Noah Alper

Founder of **NOAH'S BAGELS**
and *BREAD & CIRCUS*

with *Thomas Fields-Meyer*

Wolfeboro Press
Berkeley, California

8/04/11

Wolfeboro Press
1442A Walnut Street, #48
Berkeley, CA 94709
www.businessmensch.net

Ordering Information

Quantity sales. Special discounts are available on quantity purchases by corporations, associations, and others. For details, contact the publisher at the address above.

Orders by U.S. trade bookstores and wholesalers. Please contact BCH: Tel: (877) 811-9320; Fax: (914) 835-0398 or visit www.bookch.com.

Printed in the United States of America

Publisher's Cataloging-in-Publication data

Alper, Noah.
   Business mensch : timeless wisdom for today's entrepreneur / Noah Alper ; with Thomas Fields-Meyer.
      p. cm.
      ISBN 978-0-9840722-4-8
1. Success in business —Religious aspects—Judaism. 2. Entrepreneurship — Religious aspects. 3. Economics —Religious aspects —Judaism. 4. Spiritual life —Judaism. 5. Work —Religious aspects —Judaism. 6. Jewish ethics. I. Fields-Meyer, Thomas. II. Title.
HF5386.A2 A46 2009

296.383 22--dc22   2009930830

First Edition

14 13 12 11 10 09   10 9 8 7 6 5 4 3 2 1

For my father,

David E. Alper

of blessed memory

The consummate business mensch

Who is rich?
The one who rejoices in what he has.
—BEN ZOMA, PIRKEI AVOT

Contents

Introduction

I had *shpilkes* from the moment I woke up. Then again, I always have *shpilkes*—Yiddish for "pins and needles." My kids have always teased me about this, accusing me of living in a perpetual state of restlessness. "Perma-*shpilkes*," they call it. If ever there was a day for perma-*shpilkes*, it was February 2, 1996, the day I was waiting for the biggest deal of my life to go through.

Six and a half years earlier, I had opened a small bagel shop in Berkeley, California. I began with virtually no experience as a baker—just a strong hunch that a good bagel would find an eager audience in the Bay Area. My instinct proved correct. Noah's Bagels flourished in unimaginable ways, with a thousand employees staffing thirty-eight stores and a thriving wholesale operation. When President Bill Clinton visited nearby Oakland and *had* to have a bagel, his staff called Noah's and I personally made the delivery.

That kind of success is difficult to hide, and a buyer had emerged, a company called Einstein Bros. They were acquiring regional bagel chains around the country and had presented us with a generous offer to buy Noah's Bagels for one hundred million dollars. Today that deal was to go through.

Part of me still didn't believe it.

"Has the money transferred yet?" I kept asking Bill Hughson. Bill was the young Stanford MBA my brother had brought on to help manage the operation just before Noah's began growing to surpass anything I had seen as a small-time, self-taught entrepreneur. I had conceived Noah's as a business with a Jewish *neshama*, or soul. So, when we hired Bill—a slender and fair gentile with an intense gaze—I had given him a facetious nickname to help him fit in: Baruch Hughstein, I sometimes called him.

That morning, I felt like a young child sitting in the backseat on a long car trip, asking, "Are we there yet? Are we there yet?" I kept popping my head into Bill's office every ten minutes and pacing the hallways in between. "Is it there? Did it show up yet?" I knew I was driving Bill crazy, but it was hardly the first time. Over the years, Bill had put up with my sometimes obsessive attention to details and my constant flow of ideas—about everything from store design to cream cheese texture and the finer points of poppy seeds.

That was all about to end.

I knew that my life would never be the same. Of course, the hundred million would be shared with several partners, investors, our corporate partner Starbucks, and many employees with stock options. Still, once the deal went through, for the first time in my life, I wouldn't have to worry too much about money.

That pregnant moment made me reflect on how far I had come. Pacing in anticipation of the greatest financial triumph of my career, I couldn't help but think back to the moment of my deepest despair—a period from a different era, in what felt like a different lifetime. It is not where you might expect an entrepreneur's story to start, but it's where my journey began.

In the spring of 1969, I found myself incarcerated in a mental institution. How I got there, I will explain later, but I spent nine months at McLean Hospital, a psychiatric facility in Belmont, Massachusetts. When I arrived at age twenty-two, I was a mess: delusional, manic, only loosely tied to reality. Over the course of my stay, I slowly came back to earth. Gradually, over days and weeks and months I again became the person I had been before: fun loving, feisty, neurotic but determined, and devoted to a caring family. It took time.

In my early days at McLean, I was confined to a maximum-security ward, where I was under constant observation. One afternoon I sat there, peering out a small bathroom window through a dense security screen. The barrier seemed thick and impenetrable as I looked beyond, toward McLean's leafy, manicured grounds. It was spring, and I gazed at the leafy maple and oak trees and the expansive lawns, and I made myself a vow: somehow I would rejoin the world of the living. I would return to the lush, green landscape and to the rush of normal life.

Fast-forward twenty-eight years to the late 1990s, and I had run a series of business ventures, most of them quite successful, culminating in the sale of Noah's Bagels. As the first step toward the rest of my life, I planned to relocate with my wife and sons for a year in Jerusalem. There, I would realize a dream of living in the Jewish homeland, of being fully ensconced in a spiritual community, of celebrating Judaism fully and wholeheartedly for the first time.

I didn't know it the moment Bill told me that the money had finally landed in my account, but one night many months later I would be in Israel at Kabbalat Shabbat, the Friday night synagogue service that welcomes the Sabbath, and I would experience a transcendent moment. On that evening, I would sit in the back of a neighborhood synagogue called Yakar, surrounded by ecstatic singing, clapping, and faces filled with joy. I'd take in the incredible scene around me, my gaze wandering toward a nearby window, and notice that it happened to be covered by metal bars. I'd look out toward the trees, rustling in the breeze outside, and be transported back to the bathroom at McLean. I would begin to tear up, realizing that I had fulfilled the promise I made half a lifetime ago—to return to the green, verdant world, to build a family, a career, and a future.

So what does all this have to do with business?

Everything.

Many entrepreneurs try to separate their personal lives from their business lives. Of course it's important to be professional and maintain appropriate boundaries, but it's equally essential to integrate your experiences into your path as an entrepreneur. Nobody's life is perfect. We all suffer setbacks, challenges, and unexpected bumps in the road. Success is not about ignoring these chapters or pretending they didn't happen; it's about building on them.

What those nine months gave me is a point of reference. No matter how bad things get in my work, I can always look back and think of how far I have come.

My time at McLean helped me develop tools that I use every day in my work: self-knowledge, self-confidence, and resilience in the face of adversity. McLean taught me the value of humor and diplomacy as well as the magical selling power of a genuine smile.

That frightening and difficult chapter also inspired me to seek out the beauty and depth that I eventually discovered in Judaism. I was born and raised Jewish, but I never had much understanding of what it was all about. My bar mitzvah was just a party, my religious education was almost nonexistent, and my childhood offered only vague tastes of the Jewish holidays. At my grandfather's Passover Seders, he made sure that we all wore hats, but I never understood that we were doing something akin to wearing a yarmulke, a sign of reverence for God.

Ironically, I lived in Brookline, Massachusetts, a Boston suburb that was predominantly Jewish. It just didn't mean anything to me. I was much more passionate about hockey than Hebrew school. Years later, when my first son, Jesse, was born, a rabbi visited the hospital and asked me if I had plans for my son's Jewish education. "No," I said sarcastically, "but do you know where I can get a good corned beef sandwich?"

Looking back, I was on two parallel journeys: one was about money and products and business concepts, while the other started as a love affair with Israel that eventually evolved into a passionate, rich, and textured involvement with Judaism. I kept these paths separate until they finally crossed in ways that seemed natural and inevitable. Suddenly I could look back and see ways to use the wisdom and perspective I had accumulated over a lifetime to lead a business life that felt right: honest, deep, meaningful, and fulfilling.

Over time, I came to realize that Judaism had *everything* to do with business, and business had everything to do with Judaism. In fact, Noah's Bagels was a home run in large part because it was a specifically Jewish business, with Jewish values, a Jewish identity, and a Jewish soul.

After I returned from spending my year studying holy texts in Jerusalem, I began a twofold career that has brought together my passions for business and Judaism. I have used my business talents to benefit the Jewish community, and I have drawn on my Jewish insights as well my business experience to help entrepreneurs create and manage ventures with a combination of savvy and integrity. In short, I want to help every businessperson become a business mensch.

What's a Business Mensch?

Mensch is Yiddish for "human being." In his classic *The Joys of Yiddish*, Leo Rosten defines *mensch* as an upright, honorable, decent person. "To be a mensch has nothing to do with success, wealth or status," Roston says. "The key to being a 'a real mensch' is nothing less than character." A mensch demonstrates the best of human behavior, in keeping with the Jewish precept that all of humankind is created *b'tzelem Elohim*—in God's image.

So what's a *business* mensch? As the old expression goes, there's a difference between a "man in business" and a "businessman." A man in business goes through the motions; a businessman is competitive, insightful, resourceful, nimble, and driven. A business mensch combines these qualities with an ethical backbone and has a "shine" that is palpable. We all know such people, and I have learned that often it is the mensch who leads the way, both in business and in life.

That is what I have taught in my work as a consultant to scores of fledgling entrepreneurs: be a business mensch. The wisdom I share comes not from studying cases in a business school textbook or from poring over MBA computer models. Mine is street wisdom, the kind you can acquire only through experience, through trial and error. It is a way of living and doing business that has brought me great success—more than I would have had as a "man in business."

When I needed business advice myself, I would call my father, David E. Alper, who spent his career building a food brokerage business in New England, always operating with a high degree of ethics and integrity. He would help me see my situation clearly, assess my alternatives, and make the right decision. Much of the wisdom I have gleaned from my father and other mentors I met along the way is at the heart of this book.

Why Should You Become a Business Mensch?

At this writing, the U.S. economy is in a tailspin that isn't likely to slow down anytime soon. Millions of intelligent and educated people have lost their jobs. Even if you have not yet been directly affected, you surely know someone—a relative, a friend, a neighbor—who is out of work. As some of the largest and oldest American corporations fold or go on life support, we can no longer count on the corporate world to provide for us. We all need to develop a Plan B, a strategy to survive in these lean times.

Who succeeds in an economy like this? People with entrepreneurial skills, ideas, and the ability to innovate, adapt, and evolve. People who are excited by their work and know how to build businesses on trust and relationships. People who know that you've got to have a soul at the center of any business venture to win customer interest and employee loyalty. This book is full of advice on how to do just that. I aim to empower you to control your own destiny and discover your life's purpose.

This book also aims to set the record straight about the relevance of Jewish values to running a business with honesty, integrity, and ethics. I have been personally pained to watch the unfolding of the Bernard Madoff scandal. Madoff belonged to an Orthodox synagogue and served on the board of an Orthodox university, yet his notorious Ponzi scheme bilked billions from investors, nonprofits, and philanthropic groups. It was more than stealing money. He used the close connections of the Jewish community to take advantage of investors, not only damaging individuals' life savings and retirement accounts but leaving charitable foundations badly damaged or even bankrupt. He ignored every principle of Jewish business ethics to serve his own greed.

Greed is indeed an ugly, powerful force. Jewish law and wisdom do everything to preach against it. "If one is honest in business, and earns the esteem of others," the rabbis of the Talmud advised, "it is as if one has fulfilled the whole Torah." Truly using Jewish values in business leads only to doing the right thing: serving the community, treating employees and customers with fairness and respect, dealing honestly and openly, and helping those in need.

Lessons of a Business Mensch

On these pages are the lessons I have learned over the years, the successes, the failures, the detours off the beaten path, and the knowledge I accumulated along the way. My hope is that as you learn about my experiences, you will gain insight that will help you in yours.

Employing the lens of Jewish wisdom, I offer seven principles that guide my business life—and can help guide you to success too:

Have a Little Chutzpah: Every bold business move requires a bit of nerve and a dash of arrogance. There are times for caution, but accomplishing great tasks requires a willingness to take risks and set out for uncharted territory.

Discover Yourself: What's your purpose in life? It's time to stop living by somebody else's standards, to discover your own unique gifts and passions, and to bring them into expression in your work.

Go Forth: Don't just sit there! Entrepreneurs thrive on constant motion. Successful businesspeople always know to be ready, willing, and able to move.

It Takes a *Shtetl*: You may have an independent streak, but business success requires knowing where and when to get advice, working with partners, and relying on employees. (*Shtelt*, of course, is Yiddish for villages.)

The Power of a Mensch: Don't make the mistake of thinking that you have to be coldblooded and nasty to run a thriving business. Being a great boss and treating customers and the community right pays off in the long run.

Come Back Stronger: Nearly all new businesses fail. The entrepreneurs who survive are those who have learned from their past failures and disappointments and use them as springboards to commit themselves to rebuilding and succeeding.

Remember the Sabbath: Sure, hard work is important, but it's just as vital for business success to step away from the routine for a day off, a sabbatical, vacation, or a half-hour power walk in the park.

Jewish tradition recognizes that the Torah speaks not just to Jews but to all people. Though laws such as keeping kosher and observing the Sabbath are considered to be incumbent only on Jews, the Talmud speaks of seven "Noachide Laws," commandments that God handed down to the Biblical Noah for *all* mankind. Those who observe these laws—prohibitions against murder, theft, and other offenses as well as a general prohibition against unjust laws—are referred to in Hebrew as B'nai Noach, children of Noah.

Similarly, my own set of "Noah's Seven Laws" is rooted in Judaism but aims to speak to everyone. While I use the language and values of Judaism, my advice is meant to be universal. Though it is based in my own tradition, it speaks to entrepreneurs of any persuasion.

Think of the bagel. There was a time when it was a strictly Jewish food, confined to kosher delis and the buffet tables of bar mitzvah receptions. Over time, the bagel branched out, becoming first a gourmet item, then a specialty food, and eventually a treat for the masses, available at every Starbucks and McDonald's. (I even spotted them on a hotel menu in Kotzebue, Alaska, above the Arctic Circle!) The same applies to my Jewish take on business. It comes from my own experience, background, and outlook, but there's something here for everyone.

~

Finally, here's an important note about business. You will go a lot farther if you're enjoying what you do. I learned that years ago, in one of my first jobs. During college, I worked part-time at a small neighborhood market run by a New York character named Louie—shelving stock, cleaning up, whatever was needed. I returned to visit Louie after he had retired, and I asked how he was doing.

I'll never forget what he said: "I miss the action."

I thought, Action? What action? This was a tiny grocery store, where Louie would sell a hotdog or a pack of gum to the local school kids. Louie didn't see it that way. To him, it was *the Action.*

Now, years later, I know what he meant: the give and take, the rush of a sale, the constant effort to satisfy customers—and the exhausted but exhilarated feeling you have at the end of a hard day. Whether you're running a tiny deli, a chain of restaurants, or a big corporation, there's a thrill to doing good work.

This book offers some thoughts to help along the path, some perspective, and timeless wisdom to consider as you make your way through *the Action.*

The extremely difficult we can do right away.
The impossible takes a little more time.

—DAVID BEN-GURION

CHAPTER ONE

Have a Little Chutzpah

I will never forget the sense of pure exhilaration that I felt on Sunday mornings as I drove toward South Berkeley. Blocks from my destination I would start to spot the throng: grad students, parents carrying toddlers, retirees, men in jogging shorts reading the Sunday newspaper. These people weren't gathering for a political protest or trying to score tickets for a rock concert. They were waiting in line—sometimes a line half an hour long, snaking around the block—to buy my bagels.

From the day Noah's Bagels opened on Berkeley's College Avenue, it was a hit. The very first morning, Tuesday, August 1, 1989, I was overseeing a team putting the finishing touches on the shop. The lights were off, but I heard somebody crack open the front door and come in.

"Something smells good!" he said. "What are you doing in here?"

I was about to tell him (crisply but professionally) that the shop hadn't opened yet when I looked up and realized something: the man was blind.

I turned around, smiled at my small crew, and said two words: "We're open!"

After that the crowd grew rapidly—so quickly that it was difficult to keep up with the demand. It was as if the entire Bay Area had been bagel deprived, and I was satisfying a craving that had lasted for decades. The bagels flew out the door: onion, sesame, poppy, egg; bagels with cream cheese, bagels with lox; bagels by the dozens and dozens and dozens. Standing behind the counter and watching the endless stream of customers, I felt overwhelmed and ecstatic.

This success was all the more poignant because just a year earlier my prospects had seemed very different. I had struggled for many months with a business that was, in retrospect, half-baked at best. Finally, I had been forced to shut down the company and liquidate its inventory. Forty-two years old, with a wife and three children to support, I was running out of money and beginning to question my business instincts. I consulted with business brokers and scanned the classified ads in the newspaper, hoping that I might come across a company to buy. Nothing appealing turned up, and I grew increasingly anxious, uncertain, and worried, eventually finding my way to a headhunter who specialized in placing executives with large corporations.

As I sat next to the man in his cramped cubicle, he scanned my résumé, peppering me with questions about my career, nearly two decades as an entrepreneur. I told him about the small business I had started in my early twenties selling wooden salad bowls on the sidewalk in front of my brother-in-law's bookstore.

"Sounds intriguing," he said, gazing up over his glasses.

I recounted the saga of the natural-food store I had run, Bread & Circus, which sold organic vegetables and exotic teas alongside my wooden bowls and where I would occasionally sneak sandwiches from a nearby deli back to my desk, hoping our more health-obsessed customers wouldn't smell the hot corned beef through the rough-hewn wood walls.

"What else?" he asked.

I described how I had expanded my bowl business into a gourmet housewares company that had suppliers across the globe and thousands of wholesale customers all across the United States.

"Impressive," he admitted.

I told him about my last business, the one I had thought would be a surefire hit, selling Israeli-made foods and gifts to the burgeoning ranks of born-again Christians. I had figured they would surely be clamoring for products from the land where Jesus walked. Wrong.

The headhunter closed my folder, pursed his lips, looked down, and thought for a moment. I waited eagerly to hear what ideas he might have for me. The pause seemed to last forever. Then came his answer.

"Unfortunately," he said, "I don't think I have anything for you."

I was puzzled. Who could be more qualified to help a business than I, with my record of running my own ventures?

But the headhunter insisted. I was too old to be attractive to recruiters at the big corporations he dealt with. Besides, I was too independent a spirit. I had never worked for anybody. I was too much of an entrepreneur.

"I can't help you," he said. "But you've had an interesting life, so far."

So far.

Something about those last two words irked me. Who was this guy to assess my qualifications? I had seventeen years of experience conceiving and developing business ideas and launching entrepreneurial ventures, some of which had seen phenomenal growth and profits. In contrast, he was sitting in a stale cubicle, with a gray filing cabinet, in the midst of a drab office in Oakland.

An interesting life, so far.

I thought, I'll show him.

Of course, there was one small matter, difficult as it was for me to admit to myself: he was right. I was an entrepreneur to the core. I had never achieved anything by asking permission—or by submitting an application and waiting for somebody else's approval. Everything significant in my career I had accomplished with the same tool: *chutzpah*.

The Power of Nerve

Leo Rosten, in his classic book *The Joys of Yiddish*, defines *chutzpah* as gall, brazen nerve, or effrontery, "that quality enshrined in a man who, having killed his mother and father, throws himself on the mercy of the court because he is an orphan."

That's one definition of *chutzpah*. Mine is this: nerve, combined with a dash of arrogance.

Call it audacity. It's what Rabbi Shlomo Carlebach, the popular teacher and singer, labeled "Holy chutzpah"—the confidence and self-possession to know that you are in the right, despite what anyone else might think.

Chutzpah is the secret ingredient that has helped countless American Jews find success in business. Arriving as penniless immigrants in a new land, they had nothing to lose, so they were willing and eager to take risks that, in many cases, led to financial success.

My grandfather, Morris Alper, was a businessman with chutzpah. An itinerant peddler, Morris traveled to South Africa in the late nineteenth century, opening a general store to sell equipment to the thousands of prospectors arriving during the famous Kimberly Diamond Rush. Lacking any funds, he pretended to be much bigger and more prosperous than he was, somehow finagling the biggest supplier to give him pickaxes, shovels, and other mining equipment without payment. In essence, he made the seller his banker, convincing the wholesaler to loan him his entire inventory on credit. At the end of the first month, Morris returned what he hadn't sold, then bought it back again, partially with the money he had earned and mostly with more credit.

"You can't do that!" insisted the confused supplier.

"Why not?" asked Morris, playing dumb.

The man could not come up with a good reason, so they continued this arrangement for several months. Morris eventually became friendly with the supplier as he was finally able to pay his bills on time. The man eventually confronted him. "All these months, I've been telling you that you can't pay your bills by returning the merchandise," said the man, "and you never seem to understand."

Morris responded slowly and directly. "Sometimes," he said in his thick Yiddish accent, "it doesn't pay to be so smart."

My own earliest lesson in chutzpah came when I was ten years old. The teacher: my cousin Donny, three years my senior. Growing up in suburban Boston, we were both hockey fanatics and seized on any opportunity to skate, usually on a nearby field that was flooded over and frozen in the winter. Then we heard about a new country club where a winter ice rink had been created on the tennis courts, complete with genuine hockey nets and sideboards. Donny and I couldn't wait to try it out.

So, one Wednesday evening, Donny gathered a group of our friends to go to the Sidney Hills Country Club for a hockey game.

There was just one problem: none of us were members.

That didn't bother Donny. He led the way and a dozen of us—all carrying sticks and skates—followed, proceeding to the rink, lacing up, and starting a game of hockey. We were enjoying the smooth ice, the warm glow of the floodlights, and the thrill of sending the puck into a real net when another group of kids showed up looking to use the ice.

Donny looked them up and down.

"You guys members here?" he asked.

"Of course!" they said in chorus.

Donny shook his head slowly.

"Sorry," he said. "Wednesday is *non*member night."

They looked at him, confused.

"Come back another night," he said.

The kids didn't even protest. Politely and respectfully, they gathered up their gear, found a pay phone to call their parents, and disappeared into the night. Donny flashed a huge grin, and the rest of us played on, savoring the rink until the club shut off the lights late that night.

Now that was chutzpah.

~

It was a trait I needed to develop, being the youngest of four children and the shortest kid in my circle of friends.

In spite of my diminutive size, I liked to play touch football against my two brothers, who were older and much bigger. My strategy was to dive right up the middle, no matter who or what was in the way. It was always a struggle, but I would give it my all and gain a yard or two. That earned me a nickname that stuck: the Bomber. Whatever I put my mind to, I was determined to barrel ahead and accomplish it.

In high school I had my mind set on buying myself an automobile, despite my father's absolute insistence that I hold off until I was older. He would not bend, even though the money was my own hard-earned cash. I couldn't defy his ironclad rule, so instead I looked for a loophole. Some of my friends had boats—powerboats they would drive on trailers down to Cape Cod. So I told my father I was going to buy a boat.

"No, you're not," he replied.

"You told me I couldn't buy a *car*," I said. "You never said anything about a *boat*."

He was firm: "No."

Dad's refusal to let me spend my own money stimulated my adolescent rebellion. I decided to run away—or at least pretend to. I never lied—I have always prided myself on that—but I wasn't beyond an occasional half-truth. I hid out at a friend's house and had him telephone my mother.

"I'm not sure where your son is, Mrs. Alper," George told her, following my instructions, "but we were near the Massachusetts Turnpike, and he was talking about Chicago."

My mother was taken aback until he added, "When you're ready to let him buy a boat, I think he'll come home."

The plea worked. Within twenty-four hours Dad called and asked in his wry way, "Would you like me to call a cab to take you home?"

"Will you let me buy the boat?" I asked.

"Yes," he replied in a quiet, resigned voice.

I left George's basement, got a ride home, and bought the boat.

Chutzpah at Work

I put chutzpah to work in one of my first summer jobs as a salesman's assistant for my father's food brokerage business. Ray, the salesman, asked me to try my hand at promoting their new salt line, Diamond Crystal, at a supermarket on Cape Cod. It was early in the summer, so families were just starting to arrive for their long vacations, and the shoppers felt relaxed and excited to have the balmy months ahead of them. I intuitively understood that their good mood presented a promising sales opportunity. Stacking salt containers into a small mountain of a display, I offered shoppers a great value: buy two, get one free. I knew that three containers of salt were probably enough for a year or two, but I gave the housewives (that's who bought most of the groceries in 1965) a good pitch.

"You've got a long summer ahead. You'll be eating plenty of corn!" I said. "You're going to be making a lot of salads!" The image of the idyllic summer ahead was irresistible.

I sold tons of salt that weekend, and each sale came with a small rush of satisfaction. It also taught me that to be a good salesperson, you need a bit of chutzpah. Part of being an entrepreneur is exploring new territory, staking a claim where nobody else has one. Entrepreneurs cannot simply wait for others to give approval or to hand them permission. An entrepreneur needs to enjoy taking a risk, to plunge ahead with an air of self-confidence that will bring others along.

Take a Leap

The Torah recounts that when Moses brought the Ten Commandments down from Mt. Sinai, the Israelite people said two Hebrew words in unison: *Na'aseh v'nishma*, "We will do and we will hear (or understand)." Biblical commentators understand the passage to mean that the people commit to observing the commandments first, and only then to studying them to gain understanding. Judaism is a tradition in which timely action takes precedence over excessive deliberation. Often, it calls for leaps of faith.

Of course, that's not suggesting that you should go through life—or business—blindly jumping on opportunities that you don't fully understand. It's a statement about the importance of taking action—with the faith that matters will work out for the best. Certainly there are risks, but sometimes taking risks is what moves you forward in life.

Almost everything meaningful and significant I have done in my career has required plunging into a new adventure without really knowing what I was doing, then figuring out the details later.

When I started selling wooden bowls, I didn't know anything about the craft or the market—or, for that matter, about how to run a business. I just fell in love with the products and started selling them.

It started on a whim. I was eating dinner at the home of friends in Cambridge and took notice of the gorgeous, rough-hewn bowl in which they served the salad. It was similar to the *hakn shisl*, the rough wooden chopping bowl my grandmother probably had used in her kitchen. I was captivated by this bowl. My friend had acquired it for a bargain price as it was a "second," and I had a hunch that these bowls—with their distinctive wood grains and minor nicks and flaws brought to life by the salad dressing—might find wide appeal at that moment in 1971, when all things natural and earthy were growing popular. (The word an older character says to Dustin Hoffman in *The Graduate*, "Plastics," had become shorthand for everything that generation was rejecting.)

Without a clear plan, I drove my Volkswagen bus to Vermont and made my way to the remote backwoods town of Granville. The factory where the wooden bowls were made was run by a grizzled octogenarian named Mr. Shirley, who showed me how his crew hewed the bowls from the trunks of gigantic old-growth trees, extracting sets of bowls that fit together like Russian nesting dolls.

I was so taken with the handiwork that I bought nearly one thousand dollars worth of bowls, quite a sum in those days, and enough to fill the Volkswagen. On the way back to Boston, I encountered an awful snowstorm with such high winds that I veered off the road and hit a guardrail, nearly totaling the bus.

I found my way to a rental-car shop, where I rented the largest vehicle it had: an oversized, gas-guzzling Lincoln. Battling the storm, I crammed the bowls into the car, filling the trunk, covering the seats and floors, and seeking out every nook.

I pulled into Harvard Square late the next morning and arranged the selection of bowls on the trunk of the Lincoln atop an Indian bedspread. I marked up the prices, selling the small bowls for two dollars apiece and the biggest for about twenty dollars—twice what I had paid in Vermont.

For a few nervous minutes, I wanted for buyers.

Soon, they arrived. During the 90 minutes of lunch rush, I sold every piece I had.

I felt the same rush I had experienced with my childhood lemonade stand: the thrill of activity, the satisfaction of landing a customer, the excitement of buying an item for one price and selling it for a bit more. I was also pleasantly surprised to have stumbled upon a product that people liked so much.

In a sense it was all chutzpah—I had started a business with no particular knowledge or expertise, just a feeling that I might be able to make some sales, and customers took the leap with me.

Needing a location more permanent than the trunk of a rented car, I tried out a stoop in front of Paperback Booksmith, my brother-in-law Marshall's Harvard Square bookstore, where I had been working shelving books and cashiering. (In lieu of rent, he asked me to donate some of the profits to charity.) There, customers seemed almost magically drawn to my stunning bowls. Before long I had quit my job and was making biweekly treks to Granville to restock, selling not only on the sidewalk but to a number of wholesale accounts as well.

While chutzpah was enough to get me started, hard work was what kept the business growing and growing. I became an expert on the manufacture of woodenware. I got to know my customers, paid attention to what they liked, and developed an intimate sense of what items would sell.

The business proved so popular that I relocated to another of Marshall's bookstores in the Coolidge Corner section of Brookline with a larger stoop and space to expand beyond bowls to chopping blocks, wooden toys, and more. I posted a hand-carved wooden sign with my hours and ordered business cards printed listing the address:

ALPER WOODEN BOWL COMPANY
279 HARVARD STREET
FRONT

Running a retail operation on a sidewalk had its draw-backs. One elderly woman, seeing me with my long hair and flannel shirt, would occasionally mistake me for a pan-handler and drop a dollar into one of the bowls. Once my mother was strolling by with an acquaintance who glanced over and, not recognizing me, asked with a hint of con-tempt, "Can you believe what's become of Coolidge Cor-ner?" When my mother pointed out that it was her own son sitting there, he tried to cover: "So colorful! It's like Calcutta."

Worst of all was the fellow whose dog trotted toward me, getting closer and closer until the animal decided to relieve himself—in one of my largest bowls! The owner didn't even seem to care.

"He just thought it was wood," the man said.

"Well, it's *not* just wood! That'll be thirty dollars!" I said.

He ignored me and walked on down Harvard Street, leaving me to clean up the mess. That helped me decide it was time to move on and try a new venture.

The success of the bowl business helped give me con-fidence in my own convictions when I decided to open a natural-food store. Again, I didn't know the retail food business any better than anyone else. I simply knew it would work—that with the growing enthusiasm for natural foods, I would find a niche in Brookline. Bread & Circus was born. After I sold the store, it grew into a successful East Coast chain that eventually sold to Whole Foods Market.

~

I certainly wasn't a bagel expert before Noah's. Soon after my ill-fated visit with the headhunter, my brother Dan returned from a trip to Montreal with a videotape in hand. Knowing that I was looking for a business opportunity, he popped the tape into the VCR. The video showed, of all things, a bagel shop. It was no ordinary bagel shop. This was the Willy Wonka's Chocolate Factory of bagel bakeries. There was a glass wall, and behind it, customers could watch the entire bagel creation process: the mixing of the dough, the forming of the bagels into rings, the boiling, the baking—the works. As Dan and I sat there watching this scene, he turned to me.

"Noah," he said, "you should do this in Berkeley."

I was skeptical.

"*Bagels?*" I said.

It wasn't a pursuit I had ever considered. I liked cooking but was never much of a baker. I didn't relish the idea of getting up before dawn, and the technical aspect of it intimidated me. In my high school mechanical aptitude test I earned a 4 out of a possible score of 100. I did not see myself as a bagel maker.

However, I did see myself as an entrepreneur. To be a successful entrepreneur, you don't need to be an expert. Nor do you have to come up with an invention; you don't need to create a new computer or a revolutionary microchip or a breakthrough in GPS. All you need is a good idea at the right time—and the chutzpah to get it off the ground.

The idea of a single bagel shop in Berkeley seemed to be a decent one, but not enough to make me feel excited or inspired. I had the idea in the back of my mind when I paid a visit to New York City with my wife, Hope. Walking into delis and bagel shops in New York, I was reminded of how sterile and soulless most West Coast Jewish food establishments are, lacking the grit, character, and timeless feeling of their New York counterparts. It was in Brooklyn, where Hope grew up, that my Eureka moment came. Some Brooklyn neighborhoods are a slice of old-world Jewish life, with the look and feel of Eastern Europe and the enticing smells of grandma's kitchen back in Warsaw or Minsk. What most intrigued me were the "appetizing stores," the kind of shops found near bagel bakeries of Brooklyn and the Lower East Side that carried an array of delicacies: herring, smoked sturgeon, whitefish salad, fresh cream cheese, homemade dill pickles. As I sampled the goods in shop after shop, taking in the rich atmosphere, the tantalizing aromas, and the colorful New York attitude, my mind went to work imagining how I might recreate these institutions back in Berkeley.

The idea of a bagel shop had been only mildly intriguing, but now I had an idea: a different kind of store combining the variety of delicacies of an appetizing shop with authentic, crusty, hot-out-of-the-oven bagels.

This was what I have always loved most—devising and fine-tuning business ideas—and my mind went to work on this new vision of a shop capturing the flavor and feel of "old New York," where pictures of immigrants on the Lower East Side coexisted with home-baked challah, rye bread, and Dr. Brown's Cel-Ray soda. (I knew I could count on Hope, a New Yorker through and through, to test every detail for authenticity.)

The more I thought about it, the more I liked the idea. Anyone who knew good bagels knew they were lacking in the Bay Area, which was otherwise a gourmet mecca with delicious exotic foods from across the globe. I wanted to do something Jewish. What could be more Jewish than bagels? On the other hand, I was not in a frame of mind to take a huge risk. I had run through most of my savings with my previous business, and I had a family to support. If I did this, it would be my last attempt at being an entrepreneur.

I thought I had a solid idea with great potential. The only question remaining was, did I have the chutzpah?

*The Lord God called out to the man and
said to him, "Where are you?"*

—GENESIS 3:9, THE FIRST QUESTION IN THE TORAH

CHAPTER TWO

Discover Yourself

"When I die and face the heavenly court," the Hassidic
Rabbi Zusha famously said, "if they ask me why I was not
more like Abraham, I will say that I didn't have Abraham's
intellectual abilities. If they say, 'Why weren't you more
like Moses?' then I will explain that I did not have Moses's
talent for leadership. For every such question I will have an
answer, but if they say, 'Zusha, why were you not Zusha?'
for that I will have no answer."

It can take a lifetime to discover what exactly it is that
you were born to do. Yet the story of Zusha tells us that
we should not measure our lives by comparing ourselves to
other people who have different strengths and weaknesses.
The question is, are you making the most of the life *you*
ought to be living?

This is precisely what motivates many people to become entrepreneurs rather than spending their lives toiling in other people's businesses, answering to somebody else's whims, and being measured by somebody else's standards. The question for an entrepreneur isn't how you're doing compared to Bill Gates or Warren Buffett—or compared to the guy in the next cubicle. The question is, are you fulfilling your own mission?

Of course, figuring out your mission isn't always a conscious, purposeful process. It takes place over years, through a variety of experiences, as we gradually come to realize what we're passionate about, where our talents lie, what excites us, and where we can make a difference.

What's in Your Blood?

I didn't understand exactly what my father did for a living when I was young. Dad was a food broker, running a business he had started with his own father. Originally it was a commodities business, selling rice, flour, and sugar to mom-and-pop grocers and restaurants. Later, as the packaged food industry developed, he represented national lines like Skippy peanut butter, selling to the new breed of supermarkets across New England. (Dad wanted to name me Skippy. I'm glad my mother prevailed!)

At home, Dad didn't talk about his work. I knew his employer wasn't a grocery store, nor was it a company that made food. The details eluded me.

A rare chance to watch him work came when my mother would issue a warning that Dad would be bringing home an important guest.

"Be on your best behavior tonight," she would tell me. "The Bumblebee Man is coming to dinner!"

The Bumblebee Man? I pictured a fellow with antennae, protruding from his skull and a body covered in yellow and black stripes. Why did that require good behavior? Then my father would arrive, accompanied by a middle-aged gentleman in a dark suit. This was the Bumblebee Man? I didn't understand that it was the sales manager from Bumblebee Tuna.

Another time, I was told "the Green Giant Man is coming." It was a leap in scale from the Bumblebee Man. How would the man even fit through the front door?

What I did perceive very clearly was how my father's demeanor changed when these men were around our table. He was the one on his best behavior, engaging these men in conversation, listening to them intently. I came to appreciate that having the Bumblebee Man or the Green Giant Man over for dinner was not to be taken lightly.

My first venture into the adult world of work was the lemonade stand I opened at age nine in front of our house, on a corner lot of a totally Jewish neighborhood in a heavily Jewish town, Brookline, Massachusetts. I had a solid strategy for keeping costs down: my mother donated all of the materials. I had no idea how much lemons, sugar, or cups cost, so I priced the lemonade to sell—for probably half the price the store charged! That certainly made me popular among the local gardeners and even some adult neighbors but probably not very popular with Cousin Donny, who ran his own lemonade stand and whose parents made him buy his own ingredients.

I loved it from the start: the constant flow of transactions, the thrill of making a sale, the figuring out of the display and which products would appeal to customers alongside their lemonade—gum? Hershey bars? I loved putting the coins in rolls at the end of the week and delivering them to the bank.

Some actions I wasn't proud of. I had a rule at the lemonade stand: no clipping. That was the word for stealing in those days, and I had a sign: "No Clipping." Once I asked my friend Jeffrey to plant a Hershey bar in another kid's jacket pocket. Then I confronted the boy and demanded that he pay for it. I even levied a fine of two dollars. I came from a very principled family, but somehow I developed a slippery side, what Jewish tradition would call my *yetzer hara*, my evil inclination—which I always fight to keep in check as an adult.

My first real lessons in customer service came with my second business, hauling trash barrels for our neighbors. My older brother had run the barrel business, serving some fifteen houses, and when he was leaving for college he tried to sell me his business. I wasn't that dumb. I knew that he was leaving anyway, so I just took over the route. Suddenly, people depended on me. Many times I would wake up late on a Monday—trash hauling day—in a cold sweat: Oh my God, I forgot to take the barrels out!

It was an education. The neighborhood was full of first- and second-generation Americans who had worked their way up to a comfortable suburban existence through their own sweat. These were people who understood the value of a dollar. To do business with them I had to understand their psychology. Each was a unique character, falling somewhere on a spectrum between extremely pleasant (giving generous tips for holidays and special occasions) and cheap and nasty.

I charged twenty-five cents a week until one August, when I returned from summer camp and went to my customers to tell them I was raising the price to thirty-five cents. One man said, "That is way too much." He wanted to roll it back to fifteen cents. I had to decide whether to make it equitable or lose a customer. I held the line and dropped the customer.

One of the cheapskates asked me why I needed more money. Somewhere I had heard about a rise in the cost of living, so I told her that was the reason. "What does the cost of living have to do with you?" she asked.

"Well," I said, "I'm livin', ain't I?"

We split the difference and settled on thirty cents.

After some time, a competitor appeared on the scene. Roger, a kid down the block, opened his own barrel business—and undercut my price by five cents! I was facing new problems: price competition and customer loyalty issues.

Still, I held the line, figuring (correctly) that my loyal customers weren't going to move for the nickel a week.

Even at summer camp, my entrepreneurial instincts emerged. One year, I broke the rules by hiding a few cans of Chef Boyardee ravioli and an electric frying pan in my luggage. One afternoon when the mess hall pickings were slim, I cooked up a batch and offered it to my bunkmates for a quarter per serving. Of course, I had not anticipated some very basic details: Where would I get the plates? How was I going to wash the pan? The most important marketing challenge was that kids don't bring much money to camp. The venture was more complicated than I had envisioned when I had stuffed the ravioli in my trunk. Still, I enjoyed the commercial aspect of it—and just getting away with it. I have never been a troublemaker, but I have always had a rebellious side, a part of me that likes doing what I'm not supposed to do and defying the odds.

I also learned that it's good to have a complete business plan before you pack your bags.

Wintertime was another story. Of course, Boston has brutal winters, and like every school kid, I would pray for snow days—but not just for the typical reasons of wanting to go sledding or make snowmen. After a big snowfall, I would wait by the radio, listening intently for the announcement: "There's no school today in Acton, Andover, Belmont . . . Brookline!" My first thought was, I can make some real money today! I grabbed a snow shovel and drop by the neighbors' houses, offering to shovel driveways and walks.

The bigger the storm, the more money I could make. I would price the job according to depth and conditions: how deep and how wet or powdery the snow was. In the case of a heavy, wet snowfall—the toughest of all—I could make thirty dollars or more for a driveway. It could also be very taxing, so occasionally I would enlist the help of other kids. Some time later, local gardeners began to put plows on the front of their Jeeps and landed contracts spanning the whole winter. That was a bit more dependable than relying on school kids to shovel your driveway. While it lasted, though, shoveling snow offered a healthy share of business lessons and some good money.

Through these early experiences, I developed a passion for business: the small thrill of making a sale, the excitement of conceiving a winning business idea, and the ever-changing challenge of keeping customers happy. I was an entrepreneur at heart. I didn't have to enroll in business school or join a management-training program. It was in my blood.

What's in Your Soul?

The other part of my mission, my passion for Judaism, came much later. Coming from a family of atheists, I thought of myself as culturally Jewish but simply didn't take Judaism seriously as a religion. Yet my connection to Judaism always cropped up. In my mid-thirties, living in an area of Cape Cod with virtually no Jews nearby, I bought a used truck I didn't even use from Kasanoff's Jewish bakery. I kept it parked outside my business. It dawned on me only years later that the truck had been a small, if trivial, gesture to keep myself connected to the Jewish people.

That latent connection became more overt in 1984, when, at age thirty-eight, I found myself at a turning point. I had sold the business I had been running for eight years— a gourmet housewares company called Alper International. Recently divorced, I had also relocated from Plymouth, Massachusetts to Hingham, a town I found aesthetically gorgeous but socially cold. I was thinking about moving to the West Coast, though I had no idea what I might do there. I was free, but also, for the moment, directionless.

I was smoking a joint and walking on the beach in Hingham when a thought came to me: Israel.

To this day, I don't know why that thought came at that moment. I had never been to Israel, and I was largely ignorant of matters Jewish. My father had tried to help me wangle my way out of the temple's Sunday school as a child, and at the time, I was dating two women—one who happened to be Jewish and one who wasn't. I did have a roommate during college at the University of Wisconsin who had been an ardent Zionist and the president of the campus Hillel—though I didn't even know where it was. I had listened to his harangues but never had any interest. Tragically, Richard died in a car accident just after graduation. Perhaps some part of him stayed with me, however subconsciously. A part of me deep inside had a curiosity about Israel. Somehow, it resonated with me now.

Whatever the reason, I experienced an epiphany on that beach. I thought, I want to go to Israel. Almost immediately, I went out and booked a ticket.

I called my sister, Judy.

"You're going to Israel with me," I said.

"Where?"

Judy was reluctant, but she had recently divorced as well, which made her a bit more open to an adventure.

I have always had a sense of drama, so I came up with a plan for exactly how I wanted to visit Israel. I wanted to experience it the way Moses did: I wanted to start in Egypt. I didn't feel that I could just arrive in Israel. I needed to make it a journey.

Judy had no desire to join me in Egypt; she was going to meet me in Israel, so I flew to Cairo alone. I visited the pyramids and took a cruise on the Nile. It was fascinating, but the heat was unbearable. The country's poverty and filth left me depressed, and an ill-fated ride on a stuck elevator left me feeling more than a little paranoid. I simply needed to get out of there. I took a little bus out of Egypt and I noticed the sign as we left the country. It said, "Goodbey." I thought, in my usual judgmental fashion, Can't they get someone who speaks English to look it up in a dictionary?

All of those annoyances may have just been helping to prepare me for what came next.

When I crossed the desert and reached a border entry into Israel, everything changed. From the arid, empty expanse, we suddenly emerged into a place where sprinklers were spritzing, flowers were in bloom, and I felt order and a sense of welcome. A gorgeous female soldier interrogated me, and, instantly, I fell in love. I felt like I was home. I had never even been there before, yet I was home.

"*Shalom!*" I said to her.

She barked back, "Where did you learn Hebrew?"

I was in love.

"I learned at Sunday school," I said. "I don't know it so well!"

She was growling at me, but I still loved her. I loved it all—the language I didn't understand, the flowers, the desert. I could not explain it—this feeling of immediate comfort combined with exhilaration and a sense of ownership. I was in *my* land, not a guest in someone else's. I was home.

I traveled to Jerusalem to meet Judy. I was overwhelmed as my bus made its way through the forests and approached the city. We went together to visit the Western Wall. A man approached us and asked me if I wanted to visit his yeshiva.

I looked at Judy, who was even more antireligious than I was. The stranger became more persistent. Finally, Judy spoke up. "When you're in Spain, you go to a bullfight, right?" she said. "You're in Israel—you should go to a yeshiva!"

When I think back at that moment, it feels *bashert*—the Yiddish term for "fated." It seems predestined that Judy was the one I chose to bring along to Israel so that she could be with me in that moment. Somehow, as distant from Judaism as she was, she had a sense that this was the right thing for me to do.

I followed the man to the yeshiva, called Aish HaTorah. I now know that Aish HaTorah emphasizes reaching out to disaffected Jews, pointing them to their particular strain of Judaism. I sat in on a lesson by a rabbi named Noah Weinberg, who gave a talk every morning in a small stone room in the Old City. He was bright, entertaining, funny, and deep. It made me want more.

As I listened, I thought, This is mine! This is my heritage, and I don't know a thing about it!

I was taken to what I later recalled as the "rubber room," a small room where a young rabbi spoke to me, prepared to answer all of my deepest questions, most of them right on the spot.

For ten days after that, Judy and I surveyed the country. We climbed Masada, swam in the Dead Sea, walked along the Mediterranean. I had never felt so excited or intrigued or alive.

That began a journey of Jewish discovery that has continued for twenty-five years. When I returned to Hingham and immediately moved to Berkeley, I learned of the local Chabad rabbi and I began studying with him. I also bought a collection of taped lectures by Rabbi Weinberg, the teacher I had met in Jerusalem, called *The 48 Ways to Wisdom*—a repackaging of the part of the Talmud called Pirkei Avot, Ethics of the Fathers.

I continued to feel so closely connected to Israel that I returned a year later with my son Jesse, who was then nine. We went on a family program sponsored by the Jewish National Fund and stayed in a cheap hotel in the city of Nahariya, part of a team of volunteers helping to clean up a park. The experience helped solidify my strong feelings for the Jewish homeland.

Ba'al teshuva is the Hebrew term for a secular Jew who finds his way to traditional Judaism—often with fervor and singular passion. I would not exactly call myself a typical *ba'al teshuva*. My connection, though it came relatively late in life, was not an overnight immersion. It came gradually.

In part, that was because I came from a place so far from the traditional laws and customs. I have a clear memory of the first time I walked into a kosher restaurant when I was a college student in New York City. I knew nothing. I asked for a glass of milk. It was a meat restaurant; of course they couldn't serve milk, but I didn't know that. The waiter simply laughed, without even responding.

That's how far I was.

What I discovered at the Chabad house in Berkeley was a warm and embracing Judaism that made me feel at home. I felt drawn to this place, which was at once very informal and very traditional. One image seemed to capture that. One morning I was flipping through a prayer book and noticed a page marked with pink wine stains. It was the page with the Kiddush, the prayer said over wine. I thought, This is my kind of place.

Once I started learning more about Judaism, I started to take on new practices: I slowly changed the way I ate, I changed the way I spent time on Saturday, and I occasionally went to synagogue. It was not a quick immersion, but it gradually transformed my life.

Bring Your Passions Together

My fascination with Judaism and especially Israel soon began to make its way into my life as an entrepreneur.

Of course, there were bound to be missteps. I took a huge one with the first venture I launched that was specifically aimed at benefiting Israel. Gifts from the Holy Land was a venture aimed at selling products made in Israel to evangelical Christians in America. It turned into my biggest failure—and taught me some very important lessons. In a later chapter, I will describe how I came to this idea and where I went wrong. It is important to remember that business is business. As I learned, mistaking a *cause* for a *business* is a huge mistake. If a business isn't based on a solid, well-conceived concept, then it won't float, no matter how earnest your intentions.

After my initial blunder, I was lucky enough to happen upon a business that truly combined my passion for Judaism with a winning concept: Noah's New York Bagels. Rather than try to sneak my product into a mainstream American package, I designed Noah's to emphasize its Jewish roots. That came through in everything from the kosher certification to the words on the menu. I used the Yiddish word for a spread of cream cheese: *shmear.* I decorated the walls with old sepia photos of bar mitzvahs and Passover Seders. I served herring and genuine New York–baked babka, the delicious cross between cake and sweet bread sold in many New York pastry shops. I refused to serve alfalfa sprouts or any other ingredient that you wouldn't have found in "old New York." When one suburban store manager insisted that her customers preferred bagels with a pale complexion, I respectfully asked her to return to the traditional golden brown that distinguished our bagels. My favorite tribute to Noah's came from the man then serving as Israel's consul general in San Francisco. He called it "unapologetically Jewish."

Of course, what most distinguished Noah's as a Jewish business was that the food was kosher. Before Noah's, there were no kosher eateries in Berkeley and very few in the entire Bay Area.

I didn't keep strictly kosher at home, but we were becoming increasingly observant, including being more mindful of the restrictions of kashrut. I asked the Chabad rabbi, Yehudah Ferris, what that would entail. Essentially, it meant a rabbi had to supervise production, making sure the ingredients and processes all adhered to the rules of kashrut. Since the kosher laws forbid eating meat and dairy products together—or even using the same plates and utensils to prepare them—kosher restaurants usually feature either dairy or meat but not both. Obviously mine was going to be dairy. (What's a bagel without cream cheese?)

The more the rabbi explained what would be required, the less daunting it sounded—at least, at the time. Many of the ingredients, like fish (considered by kosher law not meat but pareve, or neutral) or cream cheese, receive kosher approval when they are produced. Any kind of flour is considered kosher. The challenge lay in finding the right rabbi or organization to oversee the kashrut of our facility.

Since it was important to me that everyone be comfortable eating at Noah's, I assembled nearly a dozen rabbis from across the spectrum to a meeting to discuss the issue. We met in the store's cramped office and hammered out details until every rabbi was satisfied. It felt like a cross between a Marx Brothers routine and a Woody Allen movie, but it concluded with success.

Making the shop kosher entailed some effort, but it was worth it. Noah's wasn't just going to be a bagel shop. It was going to have a set of values. One of them was Jewish pride. Another was Jewish community. I wanted to create a place where all kinds of Jews—secular, ultra-orthodox, reform, gay, straight—could feel comfortable eating. I had been learning with a Chabad rabbi; I wanted this to be a place where he could eat as well.

While keeping kosher took effort, not only were its intangible benefits good for the soul, they were good for business; they gave Noah's Bagels a special quality, an authenticity that all kinds of people appreciated.

Still, I knew it would be a pain in the neck—though I underestimated how much. One rabbi insisted on numbering and counting every sack of flour. No matter how kosher you are, there are always ways to be *more* kosher. It was a moving target. With bread products like bagels, there is kosher and then there's *pas Yisroel*, literally translated as "bread of an Israelite," a level of kashrut that requires even more stringency. That designation requires that the person who lights the oven be a Jew. As it turned out, nobody lit our ovens; they were ignitionless. We got around this by installing a symbolic extra light bulb (in lieu of a flame). Then the bulb burned out, and I practically needed a committee of rabbis to advise us what to do.

It seemed the rabbis responsible for the certifying would change their opinions from one week to another. We carried Yoohoo, the chocolate drink. One rabbi told us that the kosher certification on the Yoohoo wasn't to be trusted. So we pulled the Yoohoo. Then a customer complained: "Where's the Yoohoo?" It was making everyone crazy.

I began to wonder, Is it worth it? I felt strongly that it was. Paying attention to whether products were kosher helped me keep my focus on why I created Noah's in the first place. The enterprise had a higher purpose. If it had all gone smoothly and without a hitch, I might have lost track of that. I had to think about kashrut every day, and every day I had to decide whether I wanted to keep up that standard.

It had other benefits. Even if ultraorthodox Jews from Brooklyn were visiting town, they had my word that this food was kosher, and they trusted me. We had that bond, a special connection between us. Some customers who kept kosher would come in and literally get on their knees and tell me how much this meant to them—to have a restaurant where they could sit down and have a kosher meal while traveling out of town. It might as well have been a five-star restaurant. It meant that much—and that felt good.

~

Noah's became by far my largest business success, in terms of financial profit as well as personal satisfaction. It was all the more fulfilling because it had emerged not from just any thought but from my own deepest passions. It succeeded because I had discovered my mission.

Much later, I learned that the Hebrew language has a term for the role I played at Noah's: *meshuga le'davar.* Literally, it means "crazy about a thing." That is what many entrepreneurial ventures require: a person at the center who is so passionate and driven about the business, the person is almost crazy about it. That's what I was at Noah's: crazy about the concept, crazy about paying attention to details, crazy about getting it right, crazy about keeping customers happy and devoted.

Of course, in the process, I sometimes drove my coworkers crazy with my obsessiveness, my drive, and my perfectionism. I am certain, however, that having a *meshuga le'davar* was an essential key to the success of Noah's Bagels.

At Noah's, I came to see myself not only as a business owner, an employer, or an executive. I saw myself as a salesman for Jewish pride. When we lit a Chanukah menorah in a store, when I put a *tzedaka* box (charity box) on a counter, when I distributed explanations about Jewish holidays, I wasn't just selling bagels. That is not to say I was proselytizing; I wasn't. I was educating Jews and putting a positive sense of my own traditions on display.

Selling bagels, I felt the same excitement and thrill I had experienced as a kid selling lemonade. I also felt the same enthusiasm I had experienced on first arriving from Egypt in Israel. Fully in touch with my mission and purpose in life, I felt that I was living out Zusha's story: one bagel at a time, I had found my way to be Noah.

*Go forth from your native land and from your
father's house to the land that I will show you.*

—GENESIS 12:1

CHAPTER THREE

Go Forth

"Lech lecha," God commands Abraham. "Go forth!" In the
very first command to the very first Jew, God told Abraham
to leave his home, to go forth from "your land, your birth
place, your father's home" and to go "to the place that I will
show you." It's a direct and clear order for Abraham to take
a leap of faith—to leave everything that is familiar and to
journey toward a destination that will be revealed at some
later moment.

That command is a central metaphor for all of Jewish
life. Faith means moving, never standing still. The spiritual
journey is just that: a journey. The idea carries through the
entire Torah, in which the central narrative is the journey
of an entire people as the Israelites trek through the wilder-
ness from Egypt to the Promised Land of Canaan.

Clearly there's a message: to grow and progress, you need to move.

The same is true for entrepreneurs.

It sets them apart from the vast majority of people, most of whom place a high value on security. Job security, the comfort of a predictable routine, and the familiarity of staying in one field are not for the entrepreneur.

An entrepreneur needs to go forth, keep moving, never stand still.

If you need work, don't just sit there polishing your résumé and waiting for a job opening; start coming up with ideas. If you're running a struggling business, keep seeking ways for it to evolve and grow and keep up with the competition. If your business is successful and thriving, stay one step ahead of future competition or—when the time is right—sell.

You are the master of your own fate. You control your time, where you put your energy, what gets your attention, and what exactly you do with your life. On the other hand, you can never truly rest. You're always looking for ways to improve the business, to expand, compete, attract customers—and eventually move on to the next business.

Always in Motion

My own small *"Lech Lecha"* story happened while I was in college, working part-time at Louie's Superette in the Bronx. Louie was a quintessential New York character with a cigar and an attitude that is found only in the five boroughs. My job was to help with whatever Louie needed: stocking shelves, dusting the inventory, hauling out the trash—it was up to Louie. The one trait he would not tolerate was idleness. After all, he was paying me minimum wage, but I *was* on the payroll, so he wanted me to be always working.

Louie was quite theatrical and colorful, and he would sometimes pretend to dance as he swept the floor. I can still picture him prancing through the narrow aisle, pretending to waltz with his broom. "Romance this broom a little, will you please?" he said, handing the broom over to me. The message was clear: don't just stand there; do something.

The truth is, I didn't need to be told; I've always found it hard to stand still. After all, I was the Bomber, and that's how I approached life: stubborn, determined, always barreling forward. I never looked back, and I would do anything to keep moving forward, often without hesitating to investigate first.

My maternal grandfather, David Abrams, was a fleet-footed sprinter who held the world record in the thirty-five-yard dash in 1896. That's right, the thirty-five-yard dash—one hundred and five feet of all-out speed. His time: 4.4 seconds. (Shortly afterward, atheletes stopped running that distance in major track meets.)

Family legend has it that Dave—as he preferred to be addressed by his grandchildren—was asked the secret to his success at the thirty-five-yard dash. "The only way you can win a race that short," he said, "is to beat the gun."

I ran the same distance once in a townwide race when I was an eighth grader in Brookline. My older brother helped me train all winter in heavy, weighted overshoes. When the event finally came, I was so anxious and excited that I had two false starts. Finally, on the third try, I flew out of the blocks, tripped and fell on my face, then regained my footing and managed to hold on for third place.

That's who I am: a dasher. I simply don't wait around contemplating my next move. I plunge.

I have been known to leap into a project or agreements on a strong hunch without doing complete due diligence. That can backfire, and sometimes I have regretted impulsive decisions. On the other hand, hesitating for too long often means missing an opportunity.

Wear Two Watches

According to a Hassidic story, the Amshinover Rebbe, an esteemed scholar who makes his home in Brooklyn, was sitting with his closest followers at the meal just prior to Yom Kippur, the fast day that is the holiest day of the Jewish year. The hour was getting late, and his followers were getting nervous that he was cutting it so close to the beginning of the holiday. Still, the rabbi kept eating. Not knowing what to do, the followers finally asked one of the oldest among them to approach the rabbi.

"Rabbi, it's late," he said in Yiddish.

"It's true, it's late," the rabbi said, looking at his watch. "But one must always have two watches: one watch says, 'it's late,' and another watch says, 'there's still time.'"

If you always feel that you've got plenty of time, then it's easy to miss opportunities. If you feel that you need to act quickly, it's easy to make mistakes.

You can wear two watches, but only experience and intuition can tell you which to go by at any given time.

I acted too quickly when I was running my woodenware business in the late 1970s. Business was growing rapidly and it felt cramped in the small warehouse I had purchased in Plymouth, Massachusetts. I moved the business into a much larger leased space, but just at that time, business reached a plateau. Not only was the space too big and too expensive, but I had a difficult time selling the original building and had to take a "fire sale" price. In hindsight, I would have done better to suffer in the cramped space a bit longer and test whether our growth would continue.

Another time my swift action paid off. When the 1980 John Travolta movie *Urban Cowboy* proved a huge hit, suddenly everyone wanted to ride a mechanical bull and be home on the range. My gourmet housewares business moved quickly, and I packaged our inexpensive speckled enamelware into "Cowboy Camping Kits," selling them briskly at a nice profit. If we had waited a few months, we'd have missed the opportunity and the pots and pans would have gathered dust.

Whatever your pace—fast, slow, or somewhere in be-tween—it's important to keep moving.

Keep the Dogs Barking

I had recently opened Bread & Circus—the natural-food and housewares store I owned in Massachusetts—when Uncle Leon came by for a visit. Uncle Leon was born in prestate Palestine and had met my aunt Emma when she was there visiting. They'd moved to Boston and Leon now had a successful furniture store. I was eager to show him around my shop and tell him how it was prospering. He walked around like a customer at a used car lot who kicks the tires and runs his finger across car hoods. Uncle Leon looked up and down the narrow aisles, inspected the bulk containers of grains and nuts, perused the selection of ex-otic teas, and checked out the inventory of wooden bowls and cutting boards.

"Tell me," he finally said. "Where are the dogs?"

The dogs. I knew what he meant: the products that weren't selling well, the ones that were just sitting on the shelf and collecting dust. Uncle Leon explained that it was crucial for a retail business to stock merchandise beyond the reliable sellers—outliers that aren't in huge demand but that add interest to the offerings. "As long as you've got some dogs, that means you're experimenting," Uncle Leon said. "The minute you stop experimenting, you're dead."

He was right. At that moment at Bread & Circus, we stocked a few porcelain teapots, kept almost hidden on a low shelf. Those and a few other beauties were the dogs. In every business I have run since then, I have been careful to make sure that we wind up with at least *some* dogs, rotating them in and out of the inventory. It's another way to live out that important lesson: keep moving.

Know When to Say When

The movement I'm talking about isn't always focused on a single business; it's also about knowing when it's time to move on. Every business owner has a tendency to become overly focused on day-to-day details, losing sight of the big picture of the business. Of course, I have certainly been guilty of that. Part of staying in motion, however, is the idea that entrepreneurs should always keep an eye on the larger issues: when to start a business, when to expand, when to hire staff, and the ultimate question: When to get out.

For me, it was only when Noah's Bagels had grown into a large operation with dozens of stores and a burgeoning wholesale division that I heard somebody mention a term I came to realize is a key part of entrepreneurship: *exit strategy*. I had never paid much attention to the finer details of determining when to sell a business. I was always so caught up in just managing each day that I simply didn't give it much thought. Venture capitalists and other investors take a longer and larger view: Sell a business too early, and you miss out on potential growth that could significantly add to the company's value. Wait too long, and the business could have peaked and be on the decline, or competition could be eating into its profits, or any of a thousand factors could have made it less appealing to potential buyers.

I am thrilled by the idea of coming up with a magnificent idea, and I certainly am all about the excitement of getting a company off the ground. Once it's up and running and going well, my interest begins to wane. That's when it's time for me to look for an exit strategy.

My first experience with selling a company came with Bread & Circus, the Brookline natural-food store. A collaboration with my son Jesse's mother, it had begun with the idea of a store whose inventory consists half of food and half of wooden housewares and toys. Gradually it became clear that it was really fundamentally a grocery store with a few *tsotskies* on the side for atmosphere. It also had become apparent to me that the store needed to grow—it needed a larger space. In every way, it was time to build the business into a bona fide supermarket.

A business has a life of its own, and it's important to give it what it needs at the right time. There was just one problem: I had no interest in overseeing that growth myself. Managing the store had become stressful and difficult. Running a small retail operation can often come to feel like a prison sentence—with some occasional time off for good behavior.

I was approached by a man named Anthony Harnett, an Irish guy who had worked for a competing store called Erewhon. Anthony was young and hungry, and he had been trained in a program at Harrods department store in

London. He had a vision of taking over Bread & Circus and expanding it into a chain with multiple outlets. For him, it was an opportunity filled with excitement. He was going to be the right man for this next stage.

One of our first conversations turned out to be quite revealing—about both of us. Anthony asked if we had ever had a rodent problem at the store. I never lie and in this case that was important. I answered honestly, "We actually had a problem but got it taken care of." It turned out he was asking not just to find out about mice.

"You might not remember," he said, "but I was in the store about six months ago and saw a mouse grab a peanut from the barrel and skitter away to eat his lunch, and I brought it to your attention."

I did recall someone telling me about this, and I knew exactly why he had asked. Anthony was checking to make sure I was trustworthy, and I'm sure he felt better about going forward with the deal because I didn't lie about the details.

Anthony went on to oversee exactly the growth that Bread & Circus needed. He opened five more stores, mostly buying existing supermarkets and redesigning the spaces to create natural-food stores. Eventually the chain was so successful that he found his own exit strategy. Anthony sold Bread & Circus to Whole Foods Market, the huge retail chain.

Do I regret that I got out when I did? Not for a minute. I'm grateful that I knew myself well enough to admit that my passion was creating businesses, not hanging around year after year to manage the growing pains. That was for somebody else.

I did stick around at my next business for much longer, shepherding Alper International through nine years of growth and expansion. What had started as a small, one-man operation had grown to a national company with two thousand wholesale customers—including accounts like Macy's, Saks and Williams-Sonoma—and with woodenware (such as chopping boards and utensils) and imports from eight countries. I enjoyed it all, particularly the travel to Europe and Asia, the trade shows, and the chance to learn about foreign destinations from locals, far off the tourist routes.

By 1984, however, the business had reached a turning point. With all of our overhead, we were too big to be small but too small to be a major player. We were doing well, but we were not the primary source for any particular product. The small retailers that had been the backbone of my business were slowly being taken over by larger players, companies that had relationships with larger importers and directly with manufacturers. We were starting to be outflanked, and the only way to compete was to grow through buying overseas factories—rather than to simply buy from them.

When I thought about that prospect, I knew it was not for me. At heart, I am a control freak. I had no desire to expand my business beyond my grasp and become the owner of overseas factories. I was single again and beginning to think about moving to the West Coast, which I had enjoyed visiting at the annual gourmet and gift shows. I simply had no desire to oversee an unwieldy empire.

That was when I was approached by Cole & Mason, an importer and distributor whose primary product was salt and pepper shakers. The owners weren't particularly interested in my business; theirs was a financial need. A lender had insisted that they expand their line in order to obtain financing, so they looked around and decided to buy Alper International, which had a complementary line. I had poured my blood and guts into this business, but to them it was just a commodity. However, I decided I couldn't be emotional about it. A good offer is a good offer. Business is business—not emotions.

I remained as a consultant for a brief stint, but that did not go well. I traveled to New Jersey and spent time in the company's warehouse attempting to teach a group of Spanish-speaking workers about the inventory—how to tell a thirteen-inch bowl from a fifteen-inch bowl and the like. Their English wasn't great and my Spanish wasn't much better; I knew my customers were about to start receiving screwed-up orders.

To make matters worse, I was staying at the Holiday Inn at the Holland Tunnel in the middle of a hot and sticky New Jersey July. For some relief, I went up to take a swim in the rooftop pool. The pollution was so awful there was a layer of silt about a quarter-inch thick on the water. That felt emblematic of the whole deal, the entire chapter. It was time to get out and let the buyers deal with the transition on their own.

My exit from Noah's Bagels was a more complex affair, but it was ultimately far more gratifying—and certainly more lucrative. Left to my own devices, I probably would have been content to expand Noah's from its original shop to a chain of two or three bagel stores. I still thought of myself as a small-time operator, not somebody who would want to run a big corporation. It turned out that Noah's was such a successful concept, in the right place at the right time, that it would have been foolhardy to leave it at that. With a lot of help and collaboration (which I'll discuss in the next chapter), I saw Noah's grow to a large wholesale business and a retail operation with thirty-eight stores up and down the West Coast. It all happened quickly, within about six years from the opening of the very first store. Talk about movement! I will never forget what Bill Hughson said when we started our rapid growth spurt: "Fasten your seatbelt because we're going to go for a rocket ride!"

It truly felt like one. We set a goal to double the number of stores annually. We brought on new wholesale accounts. We attracted venture capital, and even Starbucks became a 25 percent stakeholder. I may have still thought of myself as a small-time operator, but my business was growing—so much that it often felt beyond me.

In fact, my own role in Noah's had become increasingly ceremonial. While a team of MBAs mapped strategy, scoped out future locations, and dealt with our venture capitalist, I became a sort of kosher Colonel Sanders, a revered figure who would show up to raise morale and represent the company to the public. (Internally, I was chairman of the board, serving as a rudder that changed our course where necessary and kept the ship out of danger.)

We had a routine to mark the opening of every new store, and I was the one who would show up and preside. We would invite the local rabbi to hang a mezuzah on the doorpost, dance the hora, drink champagne, and hand out free samples. (As I'll discuss later, we also enlisted employees in a community-service project and donated to a local charity even before the opening.) I enjoyed many parts of my role—meeting people, appearing on television and radio, and glad-handing employees.

I didn't have long enough to tire of the role. Soon our venture capital partner, Chip Adams, began talking about when to sell. I had always developed businesses with the idea of running them. This was a new way of viewing entrepreneurship: with the idea that there is a time to start a business and a time to sell it—and that part of running and planning the business is determining a strategy for when to sell it.

Before we got very far in our planning, we heard from a company called Einstein Bros., headquartered in Golden, Colorado.

As it turned out, there were no brothers named Einstein. Einstein was a name the owners had come up with through market research. It sounded Jewish—helpful for a bagel chain—but not *too* Jewish, and the name Einstein connotes intelligence. These were investors whose previous business was Boston Chicken (later known as Boston Market), which had successful outlets all over the country. Now they wanted to move into the bagel business, so they had begun buying up local bagel chains across the country, usually paying with stock options in the new company. They wanted to become the McDonald's of bagel stores.

In 1995, one year after Starbucks became our partner, Einstein Bros. made an offer to buy Noah's. At the time, we were preparing our own strategy to become a national operation.

We said no. To me, it just didn't feel like a good move. Our venture capitalist agreed. There was no money—only stock options. I didn't like the feel of it. In many ways, Einstein was diametrically opposed to Noah's. We had started organically with one successful store and built up from there. They had started with a corporate concept and began assembling the parts to make it a reality.

A year after we turned down their initial offer, the Einstein team returned, this time with a better offer—an offer we couldn't refuse. They offered us one hundred million dollars.

At that moment, the business was at a crossroads, on the verge of major expansion both in our existing markets (particularly Southern California) and nationally—in part to compete with Einstein.

In Chip's office in San Francisco I sat down with Bill, my brother, and our biggest investors. We looked at each other, and we all agreed: take the money, honey.

For me, it was time.

I did think about our employees—the hundreds of dedicated people I had worked with at our stores, the people who had joined the Noah's team and had built the business one store at a time. I recorded a voice-mail message to announce the sale and reassure the employees. I felt connected to all of these people and to what we had built, yet I knew we had to take the offer.

To this day, people still ask me how I feel about having new owners take over my business. Noah's had a distinctive personality—a Jewish soul, a community orientation, a personality. Over time it changed.

The truth is, I'm fine with it. When you sell your house, it doesn't make sense to worry about what color the new owners are going to paint the living room. It's their house; they can do whatever they want. I was proud of what we had built at Noah's, but requiring a buyer to make guarantees about how they would run the business would have limited the value of the company or killed the sale altogether. Business sometimes requires not letting emotion or nostalgia cloud your judgment. When it's time to move, move.

～

I was once sailing in Boston Harbor with a group of relatives, and I was thoroughly enjoying the lovely day and the sail. My brother made an observation: "Noah," he said, "you could get in a boat and just go—even without knowing where you were going, you could just head off."

He was right. Many people won't begin a journey without a specific itinerary: a map, a destination, a goal. I'm perfectly comfortable beginning a journey—or a business venture or any new life chapter—without knowing where exactly I'm heading.

Essentially it comes down to taking risks. Usually, making a significant move also entails taking a significant risk and giving something up. As Abraham's model shows, often real growth requires a leap of faith.

It's worth taking another look at those first words God said to Abraham: "*Lech lecha.*" God's exhortation is generally translated as "Go forth." However, there is another way of looking at the same words—and finding a deeper and more essential message. The Hebrew word *lech* means "Go." The word *lecha*, literally translated, means "to yourself."

Essentially, God is commanding Abraham not just to depart from his birthplace but to find the truest version of himself. "Go to yourself," God says, and that is the essential spiritual message. Abraham's journey shouldn't be somebody else's path; it is important that he become himself.

When you choose to be an entrepreneur, you are choosing a highly independent path. That doesn't mean you'll be alone (as we'll discuss, the best entrepreneurs learn how to find mentors and collaborators), but it does mean that you're creating your own career path, not just signing up to climb someone else's corporate ladder. Being an entrepreneur means you're not following a trail; you're blazing your own—simultaneously going out into the world and going "to yourself," creating yourself and your career.

Who is wise? One who learns from all people.

—BEN ZOMA, PIRKEI AVOT

CHAPTER FOUR

It Takes a *Shtetl*

I sometimes wonder where I would be today if I hadn't found Danny the Bagel Maven.

Danny ran a family bagel business in, of all places, Pawtucket, Rhode Island. Pawtucket isn't quite Boston, and it sure ain't New York, but Danny made a hell of a bagel. It was Danny who taught me how to make my first bagel, who dispensed advice to me as I sat late into the night on flour sacks in his bakery, drinking in his wisdom.

Danny was my bagel *rebbe* (guru).

In the book of Genesis, just after God creates Adam, the first man, God looks at this creation—this living, breathing human being—and makes a powerful statement: "It is not good for man to be alone." Traditionally, Judaism has interpreted this statement as the basis for marriage, a declaration that individuals should not go through life on their own, that the vision of a good and meaningful life includes marriage and family. By extension, that seemingly simple statement projects an entire worldview: that it is always better to go through life—to live, to love, and to work—in connection with other people. Almost anything you do, says the Torah, you can do better by joining in with others.

Again and again, the Jewish tradition brings reminders of this fundamental idea—not just that it's preferable to connect to other people, but that we have much to gain from the experience of others. My favorite expression of the concept comes in Pirkei Avot, the part of the Talmud known as Ethics of the Fathers. There, a rabbi named Ben Zoma asks a powerful question.

"Who is wise?" he asks. The answer: "The one who learns from all people."

In other words, the greatest wisdom is not to be found in a book or on a mountaintop or through deep introspection. In the Jewish outlook, wisdom comes from learning from people—and not just a few people. Ben Zoma specifies that you should learn from *all* people, that you have much to gain from seeking and appreciating the wisdom in every person you encounter.

That's powerful and crucial advice for anyone who wants to run a business. Joining forces with others is what makes it worth doing. That's what makes it meaningful and fulfilling. Sharing the journey is valuable and vital. You really should benefit from the wisdom and experience of others.

In fact, running your own business means you are all the more dependent on other people (or should be) for help, ideas, support, and assistance.

You never know where wisdom will come from. One summer while in college, I traveled with my friend George across the country, with an itinerary designed around a series of jobs my father had helped us line up through his connections in the food industry. We set off that June like suburban migrant workers, seeking out adventure in my mother's dark green Buick convertible.

In Le Seur, Minnesota, I spent two days at the Green Giant plant cleaning out a huge pea vat. Dressed in a rubber suit and goggles, and armed with high-pressure water and soap guns attached to long hoses, I felt like a scuba diver cleaning out a rusty old hulk. We also thinned apples in Oregon's Columbia River Gorge and picked cherries in Washington State, perched precariously on ladders while we tried to grab as much fruit as possible. It seemed like mindless work, but then I watched the migrant workers—whole families of them—picking skillfully and rapidly with both hands. I watched in awe. It was as if they were playing a Beethoven sonata and I was playing "Chopsticks." We were paid by the box, and these people were picking seven or eight times more than we were.

My father always had a great sense of humility and respect for people who did their jobs well, whether those people were waiters, lawyers, or cherry pickers. That summer, I came to realize that all kinds of people have lessons to teach.

My father, David E. Alper, was my model of a business mensch. Among his mottos were "Retail is detail" and "Repetition is reputation."

The original Bread & Circus was on Brookline's Harvard Street. Capturing an emerging trend, my store was among New England's first natural-food stores.

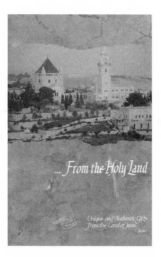

Determined to help Israel, I hoped Christians would be eager to patronize Gifts from the Holy Land. They weren't, but I gained some valuable lessons.

Alper International grew from a one-man operation to a national company, selling gourmet housewares to Macy's, Williams-Sonoma, and Saks Fifth Avenue.

Noah's Bagels was in many ways a family for the Alpers (*from left:* my niece McKaile, nephew Ty, niece Robin, me, my brother Dan, son Jesse, and nephew Michael in the mid-'90s).

I loved greeting the Sunday morning crowds at one of our most popular locations, in San Francisco's trendy Marina district.

Details like subway-style signs and period-style lighting helped give Noah's stores—like this one in San Francisco's Financial District—an authentic "old New York" feel and made the bagels taste better.

We worked hard to build community connections by participating in events like this July Fourth parade in Redwood City, California, where our 1932 Ford Model A was accompanied by our "walking bagel."

Before our grand openings—like this one, where my wife, Hope (*fifth from left*), and I helped cut the ribbon—we would perform community-service projects to introduce Noah's to the area.

An upbeat and whimsical advertising campaign helped announce our entry into Los Angeles in 1994.

I made a foray as a gourmet restaurateur at Ristorante Raphael, where I teamed with chef Domenico Testa to create kosher-Italian dishes that attracted an adoring clientele.

At the end of the day, it's all about family. Mine (*from left:* Hope, Robbie, David, and I) celebrated Israel's fiftieth anniversary together in Jerusalem in 1998. (*Not pictured:* Jesse.)

Seek a Mentor

A famous piece of wisdom in the Talmud says "*Aseh Le-cha Rav u'k'neh l'cha chaver.*" Loosely translated, it means "When you find yourself a teacher, you have acquired a friend."

What kind of teacher do you need? In some ways, being an entrepreneur is among the most egalitarian of careers. To become a doctor, you need to go to medical school and do an internship and residency. To practice law, you must go to law school and pass the bar exam. To be a police officer, a firefighter, a therapist, or a pilot, you need training, education, and credentials. To be an entrepreneur, on the other hand, all you really need is a good idea and the resources and energy to carry it out (although an MBA doesn't hurt!).

You also need people to show you the way.

Noah's Bagels started with an idea. I knew that with all the culinary richness of the San Francisco Bay area—the exquisite sushi bars, the elaborate Indian restaurants, the gourmet Italian cafes, and so many more—there was not a decent New York–style bagel to be found.

What I didn't know was how to make a bagel.

In fact, I was quite intimidated by the prospect. I have always fancied myself an amateur chef, but baking is another story: I knew it entailed precise measurements and consistency, and I feared anything technical.

So I went east to do research. There, one of my first conversations was with an icon of American bagel history, Murray Lender.

Murray is the son of the late Harry Lender, a Polish-born Jew who immigrated in the 1920s and began selling bagels out of a shop in the backyard of his house in New Haven, Connecticut. With the advent of supermarkets in the1950s, Murray and his brother Marvin dreamed up an innovation that turned the small local business into a national and then international player: they sold the bagels frozen, for consumers to purchase in their grocers' freezer sections. Not only did that make Lender's Frozen Bagels a prosperous and successful venture, it also brought the bagel into the American mainstream. Murray Lender sold the family business in 1984 to Kraft (which then had a product to market with its Philadelphia Cream Cheese) and made a fortune.

I was eager to gather any information I could, so I visited New Haven and paid Murray a visit. He happened to have been a friend of my father's from the food business in New England.

Bagels have an almost mythic aura about them, and of course everyone has an opinion—and most people agree that New York City bagels are the best. Why? I had always heard the same claim: there was something about the quality of the water that could not be replicated elsewhere. When I sat down with Murray, that was my question for him: is it the water?

Murray shook his head and waved his hand dismissively. "It's not the water," he said. "It's the competition."

I understood immediately what he meant: Water is water. What's unique about New York is the sheer number of shops selling bagels. If you don't sell a decent bagel—crusty, chewy, hot, and delicious—you can't survive. Murray assured me that there was no magical secret—just learning the craft, mastering the details, and staying competitive. If Moishe was outperforming Hymie across the street, then Hymie would add more sesame seeds, and then Moishe would have to up the ante with tastier onions. It's classic free-market economics, and the winner is the consumer.

I later confirmed what Murray told me about the water. Gathering a sample from Brooklyn, I hired a chemist to compare it to water samples from Berkeley. His finding was that the composition was identical.

Still, I needed *tachlis*—the nitty-gritty details—so Murray sent me to a couple of equipment dealers in New York, people who sold the machines I would need to make bagels.

As I sought out the right equipment, I found myself in the midst of a heated debate between two schools of bagel making: boiling versus steaming. The finest, most authentic New York bagels—the bagels with the crusty exterior and the chewy interior—are boiled before they are baked. However, an equipment dealer taught me that a steaming process very closely simulates boiling, with a few advantages: steaming requires less equipment and space, it's safer, and it requires less skill. There is a major difference: A boiled bagel, unparalleled when it's fresh out of the oven, hardens so quickly that in just a couple of hours it has the consistency of a doorstop. A steamed bagel remains soft enough that it can be used for sandwiches many hours after it's made.

A salesman pushing a particular steam-injected rack oven brought me to a couple of nearby bagel shops to show me the oven and the steam process in action. I was impressed; the steamed bagels compared favorably with boiled bagels. "This looks good," I said, "but I'm not a baker—I'm not positive I can pull this off."

The salesman immediately told me about a customer outside of New York, in Pittsfield, Massachusetts, a woman who had been equally hesitant about the bagel-making process but was now winning awards for her masterful bagels.

As fate would have it, I knew Pittsfield and I knew the woman. Sue also ran a housewares store and was a loyal customer of Alper International. In fact, over the years, we had become quite friendly. Our meeting felt *bashert*—predestined.

The next day I drove the three hours from New York to Pittsfield, where I visited Sue at Bagels Too, the shop she had opened a couple of years earlier adjacent to her housewares store. Friendly and gracious, Sue immediately handed me a poppy seed bagel. It was delicious: crusty on the outside, chewy and tasty on the inside—an incredible bagel. It was also steamed, not boiled.

Sue showed me around her shop and told me how easy it had been to master the process. I spent the day watching how she did it and soon felt convinced that this was something even I—with my relative ineptitude with technical concepts—could handle. There was just one question remaining.

"Would you consider selling me your recipe?" I asked.

Sue explained that the recipe she used wasn't hers to sell. She had acquired it from another bagel baker, a fellow in Rhode Island named Danny Kaplan.

Before long, I found myself in Danny's shop, which served delicious bagels but was rather ordinary looking. In the food-service business, some owners specialize in the front of the house—the part the customers see. Others pay more attention to the back of the house—where the products are made. Danny was clearly a back-of-the-house man, whose focus was on the bakery operation itself, the ingredients and the product. He was also a consummate mensch, a serious man with a wry wit who was more than willing to share his secrets.

Danny had never intended to go into the bagel business. It was his father who started the bakery, but when Danny had been on the verge of entering college, his father passed away just as he was about to open a much larger facility. Danny was drafted into the business to help support his younger brother and his mother. He was a very bright guy—worldly and pleasant, albeit slightly temperamental, like most bakers. He didn't like anything pretentious. He would speak scornfully of the Le Cordon Bleu chefs who would arrive to apprentice at his bagel shop toting their own sets of knives.

Danny let me spend a few days with him, listening intently as he handed down the wisdom of what makes a bagel great.

It had taken Danny many years to develop and perfect his bagel recipe, but he was open to selling it to me for only a modest fee. I knew, however, that I was going to need more than this simple list of ingredients. Danny had a tremendous depth of knowledge of the bagel business, with a few consistent mantras about what makes a bagel great.

It was Danny who taught me the importance of paying attention to "shop conditions": the height of the ceiling, the temperature and humidity, the draftiness, the quality of the oven. With bagels, Danny taught me, it's essential to be consistent. Consumers don't like surprises in their bagels. So it's important to account for these fluctuations in conditions from day to day or from shop to shop and to make adjustments to keep the product consistent. Danny also emphasized the importance of using the best available ingredients. Premium high-gluten flour costs more, but it's worth the cost since the bagels are noticeably tastier and chewier. Even on small matters like sesame seeds, quality can vary, and it's important not to skimp.

I knew that I was going to need this sort of knowledge, so I negotiated a deal for him to become our maven—our bagel whisperer. I wanted Danny to come out to Berkeley and help set up the shop. I didn't talk about the future—just the recipe, the site visit, and the fact that I wanted him to be available by phone when we needed him.

Danny proved to be an incredible asset. My primary hesitation about entering the business had been my lack of proficiency as a baker, so Danny was a godsend. It was like having a doctor available at every moment for any problem that came up.

"Danny, they're coming out a little puffy," I'd say. "What do we do?" And Danny never hesitated. He knew exactly what adjustments to order. Anytime we made a major change—added a new piece of equipment or increased quantities—we would give Danny a call, and he always had an answer at the ready. I tried to lure him out to California, but Danny couldn't see living outside Rhode Island.

Danny Kaplan taught me about much more than how to make a decent bagel. He taught me the importance of reaching out to find wisdom where you can, and he taught me how a generous soul can help another person. He also taught me that there are many kinds of wisdom. Now, in my work as a consultant, I try to pass along the same kind of wisdom with the same generosity of spirit. I always advise clients that no matter what business you're in, there is always somebody out there who is willing to help you. You just have to ask.

The lesson is this: you don't have to be an expert to become an entrepreneur; you just have to be willing to learn and to seek out the right people to teach you.

Embrace a Partner

Mentors can help you get a business venture off the ground, but when it starts to grow, you need another kind of connection: a partnership.

It was a phone call from my mother that helped me learn that lesson.

I had always preferred independence in my business ventures. I thought of myself as a small-time operator, content to run modest operations that do well and provide a livelihood. When my earlier ventures—the natural-food store and the housewares business—grew beyond that humble vision, my reaction was to get out, to sell the operation to somebody who wanted to do the legwork it would require to take the business to a new place.

Noah's Bagels experienced great success, with lines out the door, a growing wholesale operation, and customers clamoring for me to open new locations in their neighborhoods. (One guy dropped in daily to ask when we were going to open on Solano Avenue, a main drag in north Berkeley.) Still, I never dreamed beyond two or three stores.

The business had been open for about a year when my brother Dan came by to talk. The bagel shop had been his idea in the first place, and now, witnessing its success, Dan wanted to get in on the action. I wasn't sure how to react. I certainly owed Dan something for encouraging me to pursue the idea, and he was my brother. However, I didn't have grand plans for expansion, and I was enjoying the challenge and excitement of what I was doing.

Not long before that, Hope and I had taken a short vacation in Hawaii. By coincidence—or perhaps not (I have heard it said that coincidence is when God chooses to be invisible)—I ran into one of Dan's best friends, Bob, on the beach. There, among the palm trees and mai tais, we had chatted about the bagel business. Bob had some resources and was looking to invest.

"If you ever want a partner," Bob said, "let me know."

I hadn't thought much about it until my mother phoned from Brookline. Mom was never an assertive person. When we were growing up, she had taken a hands-off approach to parenting, rarely directing our behavior and bringing in Dad to handle the occasional doses of discipline. Mom's message that day fell somewhere between advice and a demand, so I knew it must be important.

"You need to bring Danny into the business," she said.

Dan was no slouch. He was bright, attractive and athletic; he graduated from Brown University and earned an MBA at Stanford. He had worked briefly for Dad's food business but eventually found his way to a job with a California school district, where he was superintendent, overseeing all financial matters. I was the family entrepreneur, but Dan was much savvier about finance, real estate, and administration. Dan was also a master schmoozer with good instincts, potentially a valuable asset to any business.

The question was how to make it work. After much consideration, I finally came up with an arrangement that would take advantage of what everyone could bring to the table. My strengths were vision, marketing, and creativity. Dan's were management and finance, and his friend Bob could bring significant financial resources. I devised a plan that utilized all of that: I would manage the original store on College Avenue. Dan and Bob would open up a second store in North Berkeley, on Solano Avenue. They would also oversee further expansion of the retail operation. I would head up a new production facility, a central commissary that would supply both of the shops (and all future shops) as well as the wholesale bagel business, which was selling our bagels to cafes and supermarkets around the Bay Area. I would take overall charge of marketing of the Noah's brand, but the two businesses, while connected, would be separate entities.

It took quite a bit of haggling to work out the details. I hired a lawyer—an expensive one at that—to help. The main question was whether the new stores would be licensed or franchised. I quickly learned that requirements for franchising a retail operation could be quite constrictive and expensive to develop. Licensing was less costly and offered far more flexibility. In the end, we settled on that: Dan and his partner, Bob, would pay me licensing fees, royalties, and marketing fees, and the two of them would oversee the new retail outlets.

Once the deal was put together, I felt both excited and relieved. Left to my own devices, I might have opened another store or two and left Noah's Bagels at that. I was already physically exhausted from running just one shop;

I was forty-four years old, Hope and I were raising three sons, and I was waking up before six most mornings. I knew, though, that Dan would be more ambitious with his plans.

It was, to use the Yiddish term, a good *shidduch*—a good match. I am obsessive about quality and detail, and while Dan didn't pay much attention to them, he knew how to manage people and build an organization. Essentially, I was in the role of the *meshuga l'davar*—the crazy person at the center of the business; Dan was more measured, calm, and deliberate.

One of Dan's first decisions was to hire a chief executive officer. The executive he had in mind was a young Stanford MBA whom he had met at a cocktail party. Bill Hughson had spent some time with a large consulting firm, Bain & Company, and had done some consulting for the Peet's Coffee chain. Impressed with his energy, enthusiasm, and intelligence, Dan asked me if I objected to hiring this relatively untested executive who wasn't Jewish and might not "get" our overtly Jewish corporate culture. Dan is an excellent judge of management talent, but at first I wrestled with the idea. I trusted my brother's instincts, though, so I agreed to meet with Bill. He *was* bright, hungry and hard working—just what my brother knew we needed to step up the growth of the retail operation. Despite my hesitations, I gave Bill the okay.

I opened the production facility in a converted warehouse in Emeryville, an industrial area bordering on Berkeley. (Up to a point, we had supplied both stores as well as the wholesale operation out of the kitchen of the original Noah's store. First thing in the morning, the shop floor was always crowded with dozens of bags labeled for pickup by wholesale customers.) We moved all of the production to Emeryville to make raw dough bagels—which were then transported frozen to the stores and eventually baked fresh at each store. This let us centralize production and also enhance quality control while filling every Noah's outlet with the aroma of fresh-baked bagels. The plant was also where we produced our line of cream-cheese shmears. It had the potential capacity to service fifteen stores, plus a growing wholesale operation.

While I focused on developing that side of the business, Dan opened the Solano Avenue store, which did well from the beginning, as well as a third store in Montclair, a neighborhood in the Oakland hills. We opened our fourth store in San Francisco's Marina district. That location became a magnet on weekend mornings for the young and beautiful crowd—folks who would arrive on Rollerblades to pick up their cinnamon raisin bagels. Soon we had trucks running twenty-four hours a day, servicing our wholesale customers and getting bagels and shmears to these four stores.

The wholesale business was never a big moneymaker, but by selling our bagels in supermarkets, cafes, and restaurants, we were seeding the ground in new communities. Later, when we would open a new store, it was like pouring water on the seed. Consumers were familiar with our brand, and they were excited to welcome their own Noah's outlet with fresh-baked products.

As much as the divided structure made sense to me, it had its drawbacks. From the time he arrived, Bill Hughson pushed us to merge the two entities—mine, with the original store and the wholesale operation, and Dan's, with the retail expansion.

"Why not make it all one entity?" he kept asking. His argument was this: a single, unified business would have more borrowing power, enabling more growth. He also emphasized how this would help us attract higher quality employees and eventually facilitate the formation of our exit strategy (a term that I—then still somewhat unsophisticated in high finance and corporate strategy—had never heard before).

Dan was initially cool to the idea but eventually agreed that it made sense. After enough time working with Bill, I was open to discussing the idea of merging our operations, but I had some serious reservations.

My childhood friend Jeffrey (my lieutenant in the lemonade stand) was acting as my financial adviser at the time, and he kept encouraging me to stay the course and resist the merger. "What do you want to do that for?" he asked. "You have a very successful store. You could open a couple more and have a gold mine. Why take a risk?"

This logic appealed to the part of me that saw myself as a small-time operator. It goes back to my childhood persona as the Bomber. Maybe it was from being a little guy or from being the youngest child, but I was never comfortable with anything that got too large. My fear was that the larger the enterprise, the greater the potential for failure. Big ships are more difficult to steer—and they go down hard.

I was also constantly reminded of how obsessive I was about small details. One night I drove past the new store Dan and Bob were running on Solano Avenue and noticed that the exterior lights had been left off, leaving the sign unlit. I mentioned it to Dan, and he said he would take care of it. A few days later I drove by and—again it was off! It drove me to distraction. I feared that with stores opening all over the West Coast, I would drive myself crazy worrying about these minor details at each one!

Was I willing to give up control?

All of this came to a head one afternoon when my brother Dan and I went for a walk in Golden Gate Park in San Francisco. I told him how I had been struggling with Bill Hughson's idea that we merge the operations. I told him about Jeffrey's hesitation.

"Sure, you could shlep along with a couple of little stores," Dan said. "Or we could take this to the moon."

That echoed in my head: We could take this to the moon.

I looked at my brother. The truth was that *together* we did have the potential to create a phenomenal business. Dan couldn't do it without me, and I couldn't do it without him. Both of us recognized that.

I thought about the potential of what we could do together. In fact, I had always been a risktaker, and what we faced was the opportunity of a lifetime. I paused and took a deep breath, then finally spoke up.

"Okay," I told him. "Let's do it."

The story of my partnership with my brother often makes me think of a popular Jewish story of two brothers who lived in ancient Jerusalem. The two brothers—one single, the other married with a large family—farmed opposite sides of a large hill. The married brother, concerned that his sibling was alone and had no support, would go out at night and secretly deliver sheaves of wheat to his brother. The single brother, worried that the other had so many mouths to feed, would secretly deliver his own crops to his brother. This pattern continued in secret for years, until one night, the brothers ran into each other in the midst of their deliveries. Realizing what had happened, they both dropped their wheat and embraced, weeping at the realization of brotherly love. As the story has it, the spot where they met became the foundation of King Solomon's temple, the holiest site in Judaism.

My own tale of brotherly love became the foundation for much of the good that followed. In retrospect, it's difficult to imagine what would have become of Noah's had I not run into Bob in Hawaii, had my mother not phoned that day, had I not taken Dan's overture seriously, had Dan not hired Bill Hughson. Every ingredient helped. I had the marketing ability and feeling for the brand, while Dan had the wherewithal to take it to the next level. He also had an intuitive knack for finding just the right location for new stores. Now companies like Starbucks and Walgreens use sophisticated computer modeling techniques, plugging in zip codes, demographic patterns, and data about other retailers and letting computers generate the perfect location. Dan didn't do that. He looked at what kind of cars the locals were driving. He watched traffic patterns; he watched pedestrians. He schmoozed with the locals, and his intuitive sense helped us thrive.

Our success at each location helped establish Noah's Bagels as a hot company, full of energy and potential—as Bill Hughson had said, we were on a rocket ride. Only by opening myself up to partnerships with others could I have achieved that kind of momentum.

Choose the Right Employees

Of course, inviting people into your business has risks as well as rewards, so you have to be smart about whom you hire.

My cousin Johanna was one of the first employees I ever had. I brought her in as a part-timer at Bread & Circus, my natural-food store in Brookline, along with one other worker, Diane, who also worked part-time. As it happened, Johanna came from the more radical wing of the family. Within a couple of weeks, she was in discussions with Diane about starting a labor union.

We were barely making ends meet, and the store was still struggling to get its footing, and along comes Johanna, ready to go on strike for wages higher than the competitive

salary she was earning. It didn't take much to put the ki-
bosh on that. I took Johanna aside.

"Just forget the union stuff, will you please?" I said.
"Your cousin is just trying to scratch out a living!"

She backed off, realizing that her political sensibilities
were perhaps misplaced at our new, little store.

After I sold Bread & Circus, I was in the process of expanding my woodenware business into a larger operation
when I ran into an acquaintance. Stevie was enthusiastic
about my business, so we worked out a deal for him to travel
with his girlfriend (they eventually married) throughout
the country, with the understanding that if he succeeded in
selling our products, he could return to New England and
become a partner in the company.

As it turned out, he did a magnificent job, exceeding all
expectations and opening up hundreds of accounts. Stevie
was a born salesman—though occasionally he would be so
passionate about selling that if he didn't make the sale he
could get angry. He truly put Alper Woodenware (soon to
become Alper International) on the national map; the company wasn't just a regional player anymore. Gourmet foods
were just becoming popular at the time: imported cheeses,
fondue, artisan breads. Stevie traveled for six months and
built the business into an important player in the growing
gourmet housewares niche.

He also became a close friend and confidant. We were
both going through painful chapters: my first marriage had
turned sour, I had divorced, and soon so had he. As we built

the business, we offered mutual support and bonded over our shared heartache.

Then the difficulty began. Stevie returned to Plymouth to work with me in a new capacity: as sales manager, overseeing a team of sales representatives. After being a successful salesman, now he was a manager. The transition did not go well. He was not well organized. He wasn't the best at hiring and firing, and he agonized over filling positions. It seemed like he was in over his head.

I faced a painful decision. He was a friend—a good friend—and yet he was simply not right for the job.

I tried to help him alter his work performance, but I found myself doing his job for him. It clearly wasn't working.

A business takes on a life of its own. There are times when it shrinks and times when it needs to grow, and this was a moment when the business needed to grow and this person was not the right person to do this job. So I took one of the most difficult steps I ever have: I let him go. We had two business relationships. He had a 20 percent stake in the company, and I compensated him for that. He was also an employee, and I had to make a change.

I was tremendously uncomfortable doing so. I made up my mind weeks earlier but couldn't bring myself to actually do it. It was like breaking up with a girlfriend or spouse. We were friends and confidants. I finally invited Stevie over to my house and served him breakfast. I was almost at a loss for words, feeling guilty and apologetic, yet determined that I needed to do this. I kept offering him more food as I explained that the job wasn't working out, trying to appease him. I thought, Who am I to fire Stevie? I was trying to cushion the blow. He finally got the message.

It was a horrible day and a difficult chapter. I learned a significant lesson that has stayed with me: never hire somebody you can't fire. Never hire a close friend, a spouse, a relative—anybody whom you would not want to lose from your life. Business is business, and often the best option for a business is the worst for a friendship; so it's better to avoid risking that conflict. That's why I hesitated when I brought Dan into the business, devised a strategy to establish our own separate domains, and hired a good lawyer to draw up the contracts. Fortunately, breaking the rule that time won me a partnership that worked out beautifully. Still, hiring someone close to you is a significant risk and not to be taken lightly.

It's not only hiring people close to you that can cause problems. Many entrepreneurs have trouble hiring at all. That's partly because so many of them are control freaks at heart. They tend to want to control everything about a business and have a difficult time admitting that somebody else should really be doing the job—or some part of it. A good entrepreneur needs to recede at various moments and allow others to take over.

Then there are the times you're just in over your head.

That's what happened when the Noah's Bagels production facility moved from the back of the original location to our site in Emeryville. In my first week running the factory, I grew increasingly uncomfortable and overwhelmed. I had a general grasp of the production process, but I was filled with anxiety at the prospect of any mishap. If anything ever went wrong—and many did—I was almost lost.

I wasn't the greatest at hiring people, either. I was still thinking like a minor-league player, and I wasn't willing to pay the kind of large salary necessary to attract a person with just the right résumé for the job. I tended to make personnel decisions more on gut instinct, without thoroughly checking out backgrounds. I used my intuition when I should have been more analytical. Perhaps I was overconfident in my ability to size up a candidate.

The first factory manager I hired was the right man for the wrong job. Edward was an older man with a European accent. He knew everything there was to know about baking. The man could have been a professor at a culinary institute. He would have been a standout teaching "Yeast 101." He was precise and skilled and a consummate perfectionist.

He could work wonders with flour. What he couldn't do is work with people. He was stiff as a board managing the team of workers he oversaw. He was not a hands-on manager but a guy with a white lab coat.

I figured, How difficult could it be? What I didn't realize was that not everybody can think like an entrepreneur. So while Edward could follow directions and make the perfect bagel, he froze when events didn't go as planned or when his workers didn't do what he asked. When things went wrong—as they always do—he was even more lost than I had been.

Edward would have been a fine hire for the quality control department. As a factory manager, he was a flop.

I didn't do much better with my second hire, a fellow who had spent many years working for a bagel business in another city. I decided immediately that Artie was the right person for the job, and I let nothing dissuade me.

In retrospect, I realize I should have put more effort into vetting him. Rather than using analytical tools and doing background research, I acted on impulse and perhaps with a bit too much generosity of spirit. Perhaps it was the side of me that always felt as a kid that if only somebody would give me a chance—if only the other kids would pick me for the baseball team—I could prove my worth.

I admired my father for his faith in people. He taught me that human beings are capable of tremendous achievements if you give them a chance and give them the tools to reach their potential. That had a huge impact on me. The Jewish tradition teaches *dan l'chaf zechut*—that is, to give a person the benefit of the doubt. If I detected flaws in people's backgrounds, it didn't stop me from hiring them. It made me want to give them a chance.

In this case, my generosity of spirit was not rewarded. Artie knew how to make a bagel, but he was an absolute tyrant in the factory, and the workers loathed him. Worse, I was pretty sure he was a compulsive liar. He told me he had baked challah not only for Richard Nixon but also for Gerald Ford and that both presidents had come into his kitchen to personally congratulate him. He also told me he had dated two Playboy bunnies at the same time. He said all of this with a straight face—actually, with virtually no expression on his face. I realized I could not trust this person to run the factory.

It didn't take long to realize we needed to fire him.

I had been over my head running the factory, and now I realized I wasn't even sure how to hire somebody for the position, so I delegated that task to Dan's CEO, Bill Hughson. I learned a great deal from how Bill approached the hire. Bill cast a wide net and landed a big fish. He hired a manager who had been an executive at a large corporation, Pepperidge Farm. He was a corporate type—smooth and steady and professional. He knew the processes and, more importantly, he knew how to manage a facility and to manage people. He cost more, but the investment was worthwhile as he was able to build a manufacturing and distribution infrastructure capable of servicing a large retail empire.

I realized that part of what had clouded my judgment in the hiring process had been my perspective. I still thought of myself as a small-time operator, and my instinct was to gamble on people who didn't yet require large salaries or who had come from smaller operations but just might have the potential to grow into their jobs. I was like a manager of a Triple-A minor-league baseball team, scouting for the best quirky talent from the Single-A squads.

Bill's approach was the opposite. Rather than hiring people in the hope that they would grow into their jobs, he sought major-league players, hoping they would lift us up to the big leagues. Following that model, we eventually made it a practice to hire *ahead of the curve*, seeking out exceptional, experienced, seasoned executives who would lift our small company to new and higher levels of performance and achievement.

It wasn't just the factory manager. We used the capital from investors to attract others. When we had nine stores, we brought in an executive who had overseen five hundred franchises for Taco Bell. Anything that came up, Jim had been there and done that. For human relations, we hired a woman who had held that position at Sun Microsystems. Eventually, we hired a marketing head who had held big jobs at FedEx and Dunkin' Donuts. Many of our executives were attracted by stock options and the appeal of our friendly, down-to-earth corporate culture.

We had two "tests" these employees had to pass. The first was the airplane test: would you want to sit with these people for an entire transcontinental flight? The second was the "higher thing" test: Did these people get what we were trying to do at Noah's? Did it clearly resonate with them? Were they on board with our social mission? They had to pass those filters.

These people helped raise Noah's to a new level, and the company's growth and success had much to do with the talented, experienced team at the top. In turn, the experience of joining forces to create such a thriving business brought satisfaction and growth to each of us.

～

Working with mentors, partners, and employees meant that I built strong relationships and brought my business to new heights. Working in collaboration, learning from each other, and pursuing goals together were what made Noah's worthwhile and satisfying.

Nothing makes me feel better than hiring people and seeing them work their way up, spread their wings, and thrive—as they bring the business up with them. My appreciation for my own mentors taught me that I could share my knowledge and we could all grow together. My partnership with Dan taught me that my own strengths could be complemented by another's. My reliance on employees taught me that I didn't have to supervise all of the details alone. We succeeded as a group—as a collective.

If I am not for myself, who will be for me?
But if I am only for myself, who am I?
And if not now, when?

—HILLEL, PIRKEI AVOT

CHAPTER FIVE

The Power of a Mensch

Let's face it: nobody goes into business to save the world. If you wanted to dedicate your life to helping your fellow human beings, you could easily choose any of a thousand careers more directly focused on that. You could be a nurse at a cancer hospital or a firefighter or a diplomat. You could consider a career as a therapist or a teacher.

Instead you've chosen to become an entrepreneur. It's still important to heed the advice that Jewish parents have passed along to their children for generations: act like a mensch—a good, decent person. If you act like a mensch, it makes every day better, every moment worth living.

And here's a secret: it's good for business.

We all can—and will—make many mistakes as entrepreneurs. You can't go wrong, though, being a mensch. It doesn't just happen; it's an intentional effort that begins from the inside out. In other words, in business being a mensch starts with personal integrity, then it moves to the way you treat your coworkers and employees, and finally it emanates externally, to your relationships with customers, suppliers, competitors, and the community.

Think of yourself as operating at the center of a set of concentric circles: you; then your employees and coworkers; then others with whom you do business—suppliers, subcontractors, even competitors—then your customers; and finally the larger community. It's important to be a mensch in all of your dealings.

Repetition Is Reputation

My model for *menschlichkeit* (being a mensch) was my own father. Dad was never a religious Jew—if anything, he was antireligious (though he did quietly collect money for Israel Bonds, apparently feeling that the Jewish state was an important cause). When I was getting close to age thirteen our rabbi informed me that I really had to be attending religious school through tenth grade to be eligible to have a bar mitzvah. When I told my father, he got upset. "That's not fair," he said. "I'll have a talk with him about that." That was my father's role in my formal Jewish education: helping me to weasel out of Hebrew school.

Despite his antipathy toward organized religion, my father had a highly developed sense of morality—a very clear sense of what was right and what was wrong. My guess is that he considered himself a communist sympathizer during the 1930s. He was very sensitive to fair play and sharing the wealth. He was also a very compassionate person and was always careful to honor people's dignity. He did not place those qualities in a religious context. He saw them as universal values—though I have always believed that they were deeply rooted in his own parents' and grandparents' Jewish identity.

My father had a sense of humility about him. He was confident but also respected people and respected their expertise. He was exceedingly polite, always careful to act like a gentleman. That made him a good salesperson. One of his favorite expressions was "Repetition is reputation"—if you displayed behaviors repeatedly, that's how people would think of you. "Doing good is not just the right thing to do," he would tell me, "it's also good for business." Dad went out of his way to express his appreciation to his customers. "Thank you for your time this morning," he would always say. He knew people were busy and he was lucky to get their attention.

The truth is, business isn't always about being a gentleman—or even being polite. Sometimes it's about being highly competitive, even ruthless. As I have made my way through my career, however, I have always tried to keep my father's example in mind, sticking wherever possible to the high road.

Do the Right Thing Even When No One Is Looking

One afternoon when Noah's was thriving, an employee came to my office, very excited, waving a pack of papers.

"You've got to take a look at this!" he said. "It's good reading!"

Somehow he had come into possession of a marketing plan from a competitor who was hoping to go head-to-head with us in the bagel business.

Certainly it might be tempting to head off a competitor and get a leg up.

But I wasn't interested. I told him to destroy it. That surprised my colleague.

"You don't even want to take a look?" he asked.

I wanted no part of it. It simply wasn't the right thing to do. "I certainly wouldn't have wanted a competitor to seduce one of my employees into giving away our business secrets," I told him. The whole idea was just *treif*—unkosher. It just didn't smell good. As far as I was concerned, it was like selling stolen goods.

Somehow, when it comes to business, many people find it difficult to resist that kind of temptation. Would you walk into Bloomingdale's and steal a dress or a tie just because you could? Most people wouldn't, but somehow, when a lot of money and power are involved, people often find it easy to lose their moral bearings.

At those times, it is helpful to think of the words of Hillel, one of the greatest teachers of Torah. The Talmud tells of a gentile who came to Hillel and asked him to teach him the Torah while standing on one foot. Hillel's simple reply: "That which is hateful to you, do not do to your neighbor. That is the whole Torah; the rest is commentary. Go and study it."

That which is hateful to you, do not do to your neighbor.

Isn't business different? Isn't it better to be cutthroat and ruthless?

If you are talking about being competitive, the answer is yes. That's what business is all about. However, being vicious is another story. At the end of the day, you've got to be able to live with yourself, to feel like you did the right thing.

Be a Generous Boss

I firmly believe in the importance of treating employees right. That, too, I attribute to my father. My father ran a successful business, and he was happy to live in a comfortable home and support his family. What gave him the most satisfaction, though, was taking care of the people who worked for him. He wanted others to do the same.

In the 1950s—long before the government enacted laws to protect employees and prohibit workplace discrimination—my father founded the Massachusetts Commission on Fair Employment Practices. Its name made it sound like a bona fide government agency, but it wasn't; Dad and one friend took it upon themselves to speak out for workers. They would investigate reports of discrimination and write press releases to bring attention to the issue; they were bloggers before their time. The project wasn't about money for my father. It was about treating people with respect, honoring their work, and respecting them as human beings. Dad always taught me that people are capable of tremendous things. An employer's role is to give them a chance, supply them with the tools they need, and help them reach their potential.

I saw the benefits of treating your employees right firsthand and developed what I call "The Fourteen-Piece Bucket Rule." That term came from the college summer I spent traveling around the country working odd jobs. In Denver, where I worked as a delivery boy for a chicken place, the owner had a policy of not giving the employees any free food. I spent long hours inhaling the aroma of freshly fried chicken. My mouth was watering—I'm only human, after all—but I knew the policy. It just felt unfair to me. It felt cruel and inhumane to put a twenty-year-old kid around food all day and tell him he can't eat. So after a while, let's just say the sixteen-piece chicken buckets started becoming fourteen-piece buckets.

Later, when I ran Noah's, I made sure that our policy allowed employees to eat as much of the food as they wanted (except for the expensive lox, for which they got a deep discount).

That was just about being a mensch—and keeping the rank and file happy and productive.

To me, that simply seems like good sense. Instead of tempting my employees into sneaking a bit, I invited them to feel like part of the enterprise. The man in Denver saw his buckets become mysteriously skimpy—surely disappointing the occasional patron—while at Noah's I had happy employees who met customers with a smile and a recommendation about how delicious the onion bagels were that day.

Respect Your Employees

At Noah's we had a wide range of people within the operation: senior management, store personnel, support staff, the wholesale crew, and front-line workers—many of them high school students or college dropouts—responsible for greeting customers at the counter and shmearing bagels. We let them create their own nametags; we had a liberal body-piercing policy; we gave them days off before big tests at school.

Within the organization, I was almost embarrassed by the sort of mythic stature I had taken on as *the* Noah. So when I visited stores, I went out of my way to treat everybody as a colleague. After chatting with the young staff at one store, I stepped out to the other side of the counter to get a sense of how the display looked from the customer's point of view. It all looked the way it was supposed to, but

I turned to the group of workers assembled around me and started peppering them with questions.

"Do you like it?" I asked. "Is it appealing? Could we do better?"

There was silence, and I could sense the group of teenagers struggling to come up with the right answer, as if there was to be a quiz or they had been caught messing up. Finally, one girl spoke up.

"Oh, you really want our *opinion*?" she said.

"Yes!" I assured her. They started chiming in, giving me their opinions and ideas. I took out a notebook and took notes on their comments. They were smart—I came away with ideas that would never have occurred to me. They felt invested in the place; they felt heard, and we often used their ideas.

At Noah's we experienced very low employee turnover— about half of what was typical at quick-serve retailers. I'm convinced that wasn't because they liked the free bagels so much (though that was a nice benefit) or because we paid so well (we were fair but not too much better than elsewhere). Rather, it was because we treated our employees with respect. In a world that can demonize teenagers, we celebrated them. They usually returned the favor in loyalty.

A Mensch Is Not a Pushover

While it's vital to treat employees with respect, giving employees too much leeway can be a mistake. When I ran Noah's, we allowed the crew at every store to play whatever music they chose—as long as it didn't veer toward heavy metal. We weren't specific enough, and the result was a hodgepodge coming through our stores' sound systems—often *quite* inappropriate. In retrospect, it would have been better to employ a preprogrammed music system with choices more in keeping with our "old New York" theme: jazz, old standards, or Broadway show tunes; certainly not the random selection of CDs that crew members happened to bring along to work.

I have also seen the dangers of trying too hard to make employees happy: it can cost you your business. When the owner of an alternative medicine business hired me as a consultant, I noted almost immediately that he had given too much power to his employees. He ceded the vast majority of operating decisions to them, and he gave subordinates far too rich a stock-option program. When I warned the owner that he was simply too concerned with the employees' well-being at the expense of his own business, he wrote me off, saying I was being too strident and confrontational. It turned out I was right; three months later, after a tussle for control with employees, he lost the business, along with the hundreds of thousands of dollars that he had invested.

Never Lose Sight of the Customer

Anyone in business knows how vital it is to honor the customer. I spent a lot of time thinking obsessively about the customer experience in our stores. How long were the lines? Were we efficient? Were we polite? One colleague told me that as he watched me, it was as if I had antennae on my head tuned in to the customers' sensibilities.

I was having breakfast one morning with Murray Lender at his New Haven, Connecticut, restaurant, S. Kinder (a pun on the Yiddish for "*Eat*, children!"), when in the middle of the conversation, I realized Murray had tuned me out. He seemed distracted and disturbed about something.

"Is everything alright?" I asked.

"It's the customer over there," he said, nodding past me. "He hasn't been served his coffee."

I wondered why a man worth millions would care about one customer's coffee, but Murray got increasingly agitated. Finally, he excused himself, got up, grabbed a coffee pot, and poured the man a cup. Then he sat back down in our booth.

"Now we can talk," he said.

Customer service was simply hard-wired in him. Business is all about that kind of attentiveness to the customer—not in some abstract way, but attentiveness at every moment to every customer.

I used a similar sensitivity toward customers soon after we opened the first Noah's location. I realized that the Sunday morning throngs, with their high energy and excitement, were also quite frenetic. It was simply too crowded and noisy, making the atmosphere way too intense. I wanted customers to feel good about being in our store, so I hired a musician to play soft, acoustic Spanish guitar, the kind of music that soothes jangled nerves. Although that was slightly incongruous with bagels, it helped to calm the air substantially.

Give a Little, Get a Lot

My father knew that the holiday shopping season was so busy that nobody at the grocery stores he serviced had time to chat with his salespeople about details like new promotions or "facings." Instead, Dad sent his sales force to volunteer at customers' stores, bagging groceries, stocking shelves, sweeping up or doing whatever was needed. It delighted the store owners and gave the employees insights that paid dividends all year.

That sort of volunteerism was part of the vision I had for Noah's Bagels, a vision deeply rooted in Jewish ideas about *tikkun olam*—repairing our broken world. We became a good member of the community—as a special kind of place that wasn't there just to make a buck but to serve as a community center and an example of generosity and caring.

I can't say the first Noah's store started with a blueprint for community outreach. We were much more seat-of-the-pants than that. It was hard enough at that point to get up early in the morning and get the bagels made. Soon, though, we found ourselves with extra bagels at the end of the day. I wasn't going to let them go to waste. One morning I filled two large black trash bags with day-old bagels, slung one over each shoulder like a Jewish Santa Claus, and delivered them myself to People's Park, where Berkeley's homeless famously congregated.

Expecting to be greeted as a hero, instead I found that in some places beggars can indeed be choosers. The end-of-the-day leftovers were the slower-moving bagels—rye, pumpernickel, and whole wheat. No matter how finely we calibrated the counts, those were always the ones left over.

"Have you got any onion bagels?" one of the homeless men asked.

"Where's the poppy and sesame?" inquired another.

"Sorry," I told them. "We just have what we have."

"Okay, just leave us a dozen," another man told me, "but not more."

As I looked around the park that morning, I saw an abundance of baked goods—presumably from every other bakery in town. It was a result of two strong forces: Berkeley's citizens love their boutique bakeries and genuinely care about the less fortunate. Even the homeless had an admirable variety of breakfast choices.

Something in me hated the idea of food going to waste, so I didn't give up. I went to work seeking out local organizations that could use the day-old bagels. After a while, Noah's partnered with a number of food banks, assuring that our bagels didn't go to waste and that hungry people got some food. Going that extra mile soon became not just an afterthought but an integrated part of our business. Trucks would pull in and we would regularly fill them up with bagels for the needy.

I had noticed in stores in Israel that there was always a *pushke*, a box for collecting charity on the counter. So we put boxes for collecting *tzedaka* (often translated as "charity" but truly meaning "justice") on the counter at Noah's. With our high customer traffic, the change could add up, and the employees at each local store initially got to choose charities to support with the money.

The boxes did cause some conflict: since we also had tip jars on the counters, there was a bit of competition on the counter for customers' spare change, and sometimes the *tzedaka* boxes "disappeared." I learned the hard way that even with the best of intentions, a business owner can run into real-world problems. After many discussions, Noah's solved that problem by screwing the *tzedaka* boxes into the counter while also allowing tip jars. We also designated a single central charity—Mazon, a Jewish hunger-relief agency—to avoid unnecessary strife among the crew members.

We also developed a finely tuned ritual we used at each grand opening. Even before we opened the doors, the newly formed crew would join together in a community-service project. That served two purposes: it established Noah's as a responsible part of the community, and it built camaraderie among our employees. (Of course, we would pay the employees for their time.) One crew painted an elderly woman's house in a rough part of Venice, California. Another group cleaned up an abandoned lot in Santa Cruz. We painted schools and staffed soup kitchens. Our crews bonded with each other and helped announce Noah's as a good neighbor, more than just a bagel joint.

Over time, we developed a shorthand name for these efforts. We called them the "higher thing." We were always looking for the higher thing, an indication that this enterprise wasn't just about selling bagels and making money but also aspired to something more.

The Jewish tradition teaches that there are circles of *tzedaka*. One is supposed to take care of the home first, then the neighborhood, then the larger community, and then the world beyond. At Noah's we had a similar approach to charity: store projects, regional efforts, and company-wide campaigns. Local store managers would compete to come up with the best ideas. We collected money to send children to camp; we raised funds for the hungry; we ran a co-operative advertising campaign with a San Francisco group that helped homeless people to grow and sell produce; we made efforts to hire people with disabilities. We gave free bagels to customers who made contributions to the public library, to voters on election day, and to those who showed us their bicycle helmets on bike-to-work day. The efforts were ongoing and intrinsic to our business. They were part of who we were and how people thought of us. They—as much as good bagels and delicious shmears—helped define the Noah's brand.

What began as simply worthy efforts transformed into something else, something called cause marketing. Along with Ben & Jerry's and a handful of other socially conscious companies, Noah's made working to improve our communities central to the way we presented ourselves to the public. At the time, using this kind of community service as a way to build and promote a brand was a pioneering concept, but now nearly every business school teaches about this idea under labels such as "cause marketing" and "social entrepreneurship." It's remarkable that these graduate programs are now bastions of socially aware behavior and good business sense.

At Noah's, all of our community-service efforts were extraneous to our core business of selling bagels. Of course, when customers are deciding where to buy a bagel—or anything else—they are primarily motivated by price, value, and quality. It doesn't matter how much you're helping the local breast cancer walkathon if your product is inferior or if your price is too high. If you have those other elements, though, then cause marketing can give a boost to your business—and your soul.

These efforts set us apart and helped foster a very high level of customer loyalty—the kind you can't buy with radio spots, bus signs, or coupons.

When the company began growing rapidly, we experienced some growing pains, and the MBAs who were giving us advice expressed concern. One of their worries was the dilution of what they called "high touch"—their jargon for how much time the corporate bigwigs spend having contact with the rank and file. Clearly, that "touch" was diminished as we grew, not just because of size, but because of geographical distance. Yet our cause marketing—these projects reaching out to the community—served to fill in that gap, giving us a core identity.

They also created their own kind of value. When Noah's began seeking financing from Chip Adams at Rosewood Capital, a venture capital firm, he saw the cause marketing as a huge advantage—as evidence that we were well integrated into the communities we served. Our core, the educated, upper-middle-class customers, clearly valued our role in the community.

Finally, these efforts added tremendously to employee loyalty. To be sure, the community-service projects gave employees opportunities to bond over something more than surviving a Sunday morning brunch rush. For them, there was value and benefit in feeling that they worked for a socially responsible company, for a shop with a soul.

As these higher things became more integral to our company, we began to develop what we called a "social audit." Just as a company might hire Price Waterhouse to come and check the books, we developed metrics by which to gauge how the company was performing in the various categories of social responsibility. We developed short-term and long-term goals in this area, just as we would for sales and expansion, and used this audit to hold ourselves to those goals.

Of course, as the company grew, there was pressure from investors to limit activities and expenses that weren't directly related to the core business. However, we always knew that there are plenty of places out there selling bagels; our cause marketing was part of what set us apart and attracted customers.

Public Service beyond Your Business

Jewish tradition encourages *tzedaka*, but not to the point of impoverishment. If a business is not likely to make money, it doesn't matter how noble the cause, the business is not fulfilling its mission. In brief, be a mensch, but look out for the bottom line.

The idea of social entrepreneurship refers to something more than cause marketing. Social entrepreneurs create companies with the central mission of serving a social cause. Paul Newman's company, Newman's Own, began with the idea of turning over profits to charitable causes. That is an unusual success story in the field. As I learned at Gifts from the Holy Land, when you blur the lines between a business and a cause, it's easy to lose your way and make mistakes. In a thriving economy you can do well, but when times are more challenging, it can be difficult to succeed. It's essential that the core business proposition make sense.

After decades as an entrepreneur, I decided to take on passion projects, helping to create institutions I thought were desperately needed in the Bay Area Jewish community.

The school project found me. Not long after the sale of Noah's Bagels, I spent a year with my family in Jerusalem, where I studied in a yeshiva and for the first time we immersed ourselves in an observant Jewish community. There, taking the day off for Shabbat was the norm, everyone kept kosher, and Jewish practices were a natural and organic part of everyday life.

I didn't have a definite plan for my return to Berkeley, but almost immediately a woman named Nancy Pechner contacted me about a new effort to start a Jewish community high school—one that made Jewish thought and Jewish life part of its core mission but wasn't affiliated with any particular synagogue or religious movement. Eager for my sons to continue in the kind of intensive Jewish environment we had just experienced in Israel, I was enthusiastic about the plan, with one caveat: "My son is entering sixth grade," I said. "We need to have this up and running in three years."

I did not sign on right away, fearing it was going to be too much philosophy and not enough *tachlis* (brass tacks). I wasn't sure it was the right project for me. Eventually, seeing it really start to take shape, I agreed to serve as president of the board, with an unusual arrangement. I had always been an independent entrepreneur, not an organization man. I agreed to serve as president but asked that another board member chair the meetings. It was unusual but it worked. Even beyond the nuts and bolts of running meetings, the job was a serious challenge. In part, I am simply not a political creature. I don't hide my feelings; I'm not so skilled at forming alliances. One reason I enjoy being an entrepreneur is the freedom it offers from office politics.

Of course, I *am* a salesman, and that was a big part of the job. That first year took all of my talents to sell what was essentially a dream. Prospective parents would ask, "How many students will there be?" "Thirty, fifty, eighty," I would answer, selling an evolving vision. We needed so many pieces: the students, the head of the school, the building, the curriculum, the approach—and of course, the money. I developed more patience and negotiating skill than I ever thought I was capable of learning.

The biggest challenge was keeping the group focused on the goal. I was afraid we could sit and talk forever. I had little tolerance for long detours or digressions. I just tried to keep the ball rolling forward. We had a timeline to follow.

The Jewish Community High School of the Bay opened its doors—albeit in a small converted kindergarten building in Marin County—in 2001, three years after my first conversation with Nancy. In the interim, it had become a full-time volunteer job for me, one of the most challenging I had ever tackled. We raised enough money to build our own campus, a gorgeous facility in San Francisco that opened the next year.

The night of my son David's high school graduation in 2005 was one of the highlights of my life. I sat on the stage next to Nancy. I don't think I have ever felt as proud and grateful in my life as I did that afternoon, watching my son and his classmates march across the stage in their caps and gowns, fulfilling the dream of so many people who worked to create the school. I felt humbled and thankful, seeing the fruits of my labors pay off so beautifully.

When I tell people that helping to create the high school is my proudest accomplishment, sometimes they don't believe me. After all, I ran a business that was the nation's largest kosher retailer and then sold it for millions. This was different. This was the fulfillment of a vision, and it was about creating the future. I had helped create an opportunity for my sons and others to have the kind of integrated Jewish education we had dreamed about.

If helping to build the school was my contribution to the Jewish future, my next move was an attempt to help enhance the Jewish *present*. For a long time I had felt that a key piece of Jewish infrastructure was missing from the Bay Area: a high quality kosher restaurant. I'm not talking about a deli or a hotdog stand. What I envisioned was a fabulous, white-tablecloth establishment that just happened to be kosher. I saw it not only as a profit center but also as a gathering place where people from all segments of the Bay Area Jewish world would come together. I knew such a restaurant would also act as a magnet, helping to attract traditional, community-minded Jews to the area.

At first, I considered Middle Eastern food and then had an idea for a Chinese rice-bowl restaurant. I settled on Italian food, partnering with an Italian-born chef who had run a successful restaurant in Walnut Creek. We decided to make the menu pescetarian—that is, a dairy selection as well as fish but not meat—in order to draw in Berkeley's healthy eaters in addition to the kosher crowd. It was a traditional Italian menu with a lighter touch than one finds in old-school Italian restaurants. I found seven other investors, all people who shared my vision of creating a community institution.

Ristorante Raphael—named for both the Biblical angel and the Italian artist—opened in the summer of 2003 on a busy block not far from the UC Berkeley campus, and I was pleased that it did indeed become a center of community life, a gathering place where the common denominator was great kosher food. Raphael hosted weddings and a Jewish film festival; Jewish groups would hold their meetings at its tables; a group of Jewish professors used it as a regular gathering spot.

It also proved a wonderful family enterprise, with Hope doing a superb job managing the catering department. We catered weddings, bar and bat mitzvahs, school dinners, and university events. We also provided food for meetings of Jewish community organizations and even single meals for kosher business travelers. Family businesses can be deeply problematic, but in this case it worked, mostly because our roles were so clearly separate and defined.

Raphael lasted four years. It hovered around the break-even point, but it never made a profit. I was disappointed to see it go, as were the restaurant's many fans and regulars. As I discussed earlier, though, it's vital for an entrepreneur to know when to get out. The neighborhood was changing, and many shops were closing in downtown Berkeley.

There are some factors an entrepreneur can't control, but it's important to face up to reality. It doesn't make sense to continue to pour money into a marginal proposition. Still, I was proud of what I had created and grateful for all of the wonderful times at Raphael.

~

Businesses come and go, and ultimately so do people. What's left are our deeds, our memory.

"Who is honored?" Ben Zoma asks in the Mishna. His answer was this: "The one who honors others." That, in the end, is what being a mensch is all about: living a life that honors others. Ben Zoma's wisdom is so basic as to seem simple, yet it strikes me as a profound insight. You (and your business) don't earn the respect of people—and customers—by pursuing respect. You earn it through the way you treat others, through honoring everyone around you—by being a mensch every day.

Rock is strong, but iron breaks it.
Iron is strong, but fire melts it.
Fire is strong, but water extinguishes it.
Water is strong, but the clouds carry it.
The clouds are strong, but the wind drives them.
The wind is strong, but man withstands it.

—TALMUD

CHAPTER SIX

Come Back Stronger

The vast majority of new businesses fail. That's a reality of being an entrepreneur. No matter how good the idea might seem, no matter how loyal your customers are, no matter how promising the market appears, success very often just doesn't last. A stronger competitor comes along. The block where you located your restaurant changes. Suddenly your product just isn't popular anymore for reasons of fashion or fickle markets or changing technology.

Businesses come and go, yet successful entrepreneurs survive by adapting to changing circumstances while maintaining their core values. Adapting yet keeping the faith has made Jews the quintessential survivors.

In his famous essay "Israel: The Ever-Dying People," the great Jewish thinker Simon Rawidowicz argued that nearly every generation of Jews has perceived itself as the last. Each generation has faced threats both external (persecution, pogroms, crusades, expulsion) and internal (assimilation, intermarriage, ignorance, infighting) so that fear of the end has become an integral part of Judaism. "If we are the last," wrote Rawidowicz, "let us be the last as our fathers and forefathers were. Let us prepare the ground for the last Jews who will come after us, and for the last Jews who will rise after them, and so on until the end of days."

That is surely the ultimate Jewish irony: it may well be that the perennial anxiety about survival is exactly what has kept the Jewish people alive. Surely oppressors have come close to destroying the Jewish people—most tragically in the Holocaust. Yet each generation has found ways to survive by innovating and adapting while staying true to Judaism's essence.

Every entrepreneur (of any faith) can learn from that quality. In business, you simply cannot be stagnant, nor can you thrive by solving yesterday's problems. You must constantly adapt to current realities. The greatest threat is hubris—coming to believe that you are or your business is invincible and eternal.

Lessons of Your Darkest Hour

I entered the University of Wisconsin as a transfer student in the spring of 1968, at the height of the protest movement against the Vietnam War. The protests had so rocked the Madison campus that it sometimes felt as if we were the ones living in a war zone. Before that year, I had never been particularly political, but the cause spoke to me and brought out my activist side. I was majoring in economics and became involved with a group of students intent on confronting a professor some of us suspected of working for the CIA. Like many of my peers, I was smoking marijuana almost every day and also indulged in mescaline and twice in LSD.

I knew that I was due to be drafted as soon as I graduated, and that filled me with anxiety. Life got increasingly wild, both inside and outside. One of my roommates even kept a pet bat in the house. I witnessed disturbing scenes seemingly daily—police using clubs to beat protesters, organizers talking about cutting telephone lines and blowing up trains heading to a local munitions plant.

Amidst the tumult, I also faced a decision: when I got my degree, would I return to Brookline to join my father's food business, or would I carry out my new vision of becoming a left-wing provocateur preaching the revolution? I had no clue where I was headed.

With all of the disarray inside and out, I lost control.

By May of 1969, I entered a kind of persistent mania, not sleeping for many nights, intentionally ignoring my studies, and driving a taxi to earn money. I began experiencing hallucinations, hearing voices, and seeing a recurrent vision of clean sheets on tucked-in and orderly beds. Amid the chaos, some part of me was yearning for order.

This all came to a head one evening when, at the encouragement of my roommate, I telephoned my parents back in Brookline. When my father picked up, I'm sure he recognized my voice but not the person who was speaking to him.

"We've got to get to Nixon and talk some sense into him!" I told my father. "You know people in Washington, don't you?" I had become so detached from reality that I somehow felt the future of the world was in my own hands. Was I the Messiah?

My parents knew right away something was very wrong. The next day they flew to Madison and checked into a nice hotel, where I paid a visit. It was a bizarre meeting: my buttoned-down, suburban parents in their luxurious lakefront hotel room faced me—unkempt, unshaven, and out of control. My mother tried to clean me up, even clipping my toenails while my father patiently listened to my increasingly bizarre pleas about contacting the president.

Wisely, he did not argue; he just followed his instinct to get me out of Madison.

"Let's go back to Boston first," he said. "And then we'll work on that."

My parents had relocated from our family home to a penthouse apartment in the Coolidge Corner section of Brookline. I slept in a spare bedroom, where my brother-in-law Marshall spent the night watching me, lest I do damage to myself or someone else. I felt frantic, scared, vulnerable, and self-assured, all at the same time.

The next morning, Dad took me to the home of a family friend I'll call "Dr. Morrie." Morrie was a geriatric psychiatrist. It seems ludicrous, looking back—a professional who was trained in doling out advice and medications for blue-haired septuagenarians trying to make sense of a ranting flipped-out campus radical—but perhaps Morrie was the only mental-health professional my parents knew.

An additional advantage from the point of view of my father—who was likely deeply embarrassed by me at that moment—was that Morrie had a private home office, a pine-paneled study in the basement of his suburban home. The whole scene—and the contrast with my Madison campus—made me feel even more agitated. The war was raging in Vietnam, the world was falling apart, and here was Morrie smoking his pipe, playing golf, and gently nodding and murmuring "Uh huh . . . " to patients in his Newton home office.

What happened next provoked a response. Perhaps it was my reaction to the absurdity of the situation, or maybe I was trying to "radicalize" Morrie. Whatever the reason, I began to slowly disrobe. I was a salesman. I was trying to sell Morrie on the idea that he needed to get in touch with his real emotions. Poor guy, the geriatric psychiatrist nearing retirement was facing a naked hippie in his basement.

Morrie was not amused. In fact, he decided I was dangerous and urged my father to send me away.

My father drove me back to the apartment in silence. The next morning a police squad car showed up.

I asked why the cops were there.

"They're going to take us to see a doctor," Dad said.

For whatever reason, that made sense to me, and I got into the car, chatting amiably with the officers and offering them a copy of the Buddhist guidebook *Zen Flesh, Zen Bones*. They were polite. Twenty minutes later, we arrived at the gates of what appeared to be the manicured grounds of an upscale New England prep school. It turned out to be McLean Hospital.

"What's going on here?" I asked as the police escorted me from the car.

They didn't answer, and I didn't resist. I knew my father had arranged this, and I trusted him implicitly. I was brought to the Quiet Room, an observation area with a thick door and no furniture. Scared, confused, and anxious, I didn't know if the scene was real or if I was somehow imagining it.

Soon, another patient approached me. I learned later that he was a biochemistry professor at a local college, an older Jewish gentleman who was the self-appointed rabbi of the ward. He was a warm, chain-smoking little man who ranted about physics and the Torah, but his warmth and willingness to reach out to me made me feel that I would be okay.

My memory of what happened next is hazy, probably because the doctors soon put me on psychotropic medications—mostly Thorazine, which completely knocked me out. It was like being in a fog machine, like wearing psychological handcuffs. I came to understand that I could not leave this place. I was stuck here. I also came to realize, within a few days, where I was—that this was a mental hospital.

I told anyone who would listen that I wanted to leave— that I just needed to get down to my parents' place on Cape Cod to get some rest. My repeated requests didn't get much response from the authorities. After a week they did move me from the maximum-security building to a more open ward. I learned that I would be there for a month before I got my prognosis.

At that point, probably because of the Thorazine, I had undergone a dramatic shift from manic to depressed—or at least knocked out. Days earlier in Madison, I had been staying up all night raving about revolution. Now I was practically a zombie.

At McLean I began attending group therapy, but I felt strongly that I didn't fit in. I did not think I was like the crazy people surrounding me. Clearly, they all belonged here, I thought, but not me. It took time—weeks and months—for me to come to the realization that, yes, I was one of them. Over time, my eagerness to leave subsided. I became more resigned. The weeks became months.

I never became emotionally close to anyone at McLean except for Irving, the professor. I filled my time with the small tasks—sewing wallets or painting walls—that were assigned as occupational therapy. I hated the work and felt terribly bored. Over time, my doctors and therapists worked out a multistep plan for my gradual reintegration into society. At first I was allowed to go to the cafeteria by myself, then to the library, then out onto the grounds. Some inmates even left the grounds and worked away from the hospital, returning at night.

I spent nine months at McLean. (In later years I came to wonder whether McLean kept me longer than necessary because my family had the means to pay.) While I resented the restrictions and the separation from the world outside, I came to think of it as a healthy postgraduate experience. I was forced to examine myself under a microscope—to confront issues with my parents, with females, and with other hang-ups. Before McLean, I was bottled up, nervous, anxious, and explosive. Through my experiences there, I learned to open up, to deal better with my emotions and feelings, and to face the deepest issues as they arose in my life. That helped me calm down and prepared me to face life in a healthy way.

I could not leave without a plan. That was the rule. So, together with my therapists and my parents, I devised one—albeit not a very ambitious one. I would live with my parents and work for my brother-in-law.

In March of 1970 I was released from McLean, hardly whole but surely healthier than the wild-eyed version of myself that had phoned my parents nine months earlier. I was well enough to go home, settle down, and begin to find my way.

You Can Bounce Back

While my experience that year is never far from my mind, I am grateful that I have never come close to revisiting it in the decades since. I certainly experience mood swings, but I now have the tools to moderate them.

I often think back on those nine months and wonder what happened to me—what caused my manic break and how the experience changed me. McLean gave me an understanding that people are very complex. Most of us tend to size others up quickly and make snap judgments that dictate our actions. McLean made me more aware of the complexities and contradictions in people. I came to understand that actions are often driven by powerful motivations far beneath the surface. McLean taught me that you can survive even the challenges that once seemed insurmountable. It helped me realize my own ability to bounce back and the remarkable resilience of the human mind and spirit.

I carry those lessons with me, daily reminders of the preciousness of life, the fragility of the human mind, and the vicarious nature of our existence. That has made me a more compassionate employer. At Noah's Bagels and my other businesses, I frequently had to manage employees with personality quirks, insecurities, and fragile psyches.

I liked to visit at odd hours, mostly to schmooze with the night bakers and help to boost morale. One night I walked into one of the stores during the graveyard shift, only to hear a strange moaning sound. Not wanting to frighten the night baker, I called out from the door, "Bruce, is that damn oven acting up again?" Then I walked in, discovering Bruce in orange robes, his head newly shaved. Bruce had occasional bouts with alcoholism and frequently reacted by taking on extreme changes in behavior. The sound I had heard was Tibetan Buddhist chanting.

"I'm not Bruce anymore," he told me. "I'm Sanjay."

I valued Bruce as an employee, and if he wanted to be Sanjay with orange robes and chanting, who was I to tell him differently? I acted as if nothing out of the ordinary had happened, sampled a bagel, and wished him good night. I'm sure he appreciated my nonchalance, as he remained a dedicated and valuable worker.

At Alper International, I had an excellent bookkeeper who was friendly, accurate, and quick. Then I sensed that something had changed and became suspicious of her, eventually discovering that Candy had forged my name on checks totaling thousands of dollars. I confronted her, threatening to alert the police unless she repaid me immediately. Candy admitted her problem: she had become addicted to cocaine but was in treatment to overcome her addiction. On the spot, Candy wrote me two years' worth of postdated checks to repay the money. I fired her but accepted the checks, promising to take no further action unless one of the checks bounced. None did, and after two years, she sent a lovely note thanking me for my trust and informing me that she had turned her life around, in part because I believed in her.

The Talmud tells us "*Dan l'chaf zechut*"—judge a person favorably. I was known for giving my workers the benefit of the doubt. I'm sure that tendency to understand and be comfortable with personality quirks came in part from my McLean experience.

A Failed Business Can Be a New Beginning

Years after McLean, the perspective I gained would prove tremendously valuable in helping me to cope with my one significant failure as an entrepreneur. That chapter began after I returned from my second visit to Israel, flush with excitement about Zionism and eager to find professional opportunities that might also benefit the Jewish homeland. I heard on a radio broadcast that a huge proportion of Americans—30 percent—had experienced a born-again conversion. Jerry Falwell had become a household name, and more and more Americans were drawn to evangelical Christianity.

I couldn't get that startling statistic out of my mind: nearly one hundred million people had become born-again Christians. Suddenly it struck me that this might be a way for me to do something for Israel. I knew that many

Christians were fascinated with the Holy Land. How about selling Israeli products to them? It seemed so obvious that I wondered why nobody else had thought of it. (That should have been my first tip-off!) Since I had spent more than a dozen years in the gift business—much of it selling imported products—I thought, Who better than I to start such a business?

My mind was racing, and I felt the buzz I always experience when I'm in the process of devising a new business idea. The right idea at the right time with the right ingredients and execution can have unlimited potential, and this idea felt like a winner.

I had always done best when I felt true passion for the business I was running. This idea seemed a natural: it combined my knowledge of importing and marketing gifts, my passion for Israel, and a major cultural trend. How could I go wrong?

There's an old Israeli joke that I hadn't heard at the time but that I was about to learn the hard way: How do you make a small fortune in Israel? Start with a large one.

I began by selling a line of Israeli food products to supermarkets, primarily in Southern California and the Bible Belt. I tried to get foods that were mainstream enough that people understood them but special because of where they were from. My pitch: "Special foods from a special place." I would find the best crackers, the tastiest jam, and the purest mineral water Israel could offer, emphasizing that these foods were different because they came from the

Holy Land, the land where Jesus walked and breathed and taught.

I quickly encountered problems. I opened one sample shipment of crackers, only to find that each box had a microscopic hole in the cellophane, rendering the crackers stale. Quality control posed a major challenge. Then there were the products themselves. While Americans were becoming more aware of ingredients in food and pursuing healthier diets, many of these Israeli foods were loaded with sugar and preservatives.

I decided that instead of supermarkets, I would market through a mail-order catalogue. Marketing the foods in a catalog proved much more difficult than I anticipated. I never solved the challenges of quality control and shelf life. I shifted focus again, moving from foods to giftware. From my experience with Alper International, I knew about the gift business even more than food. I began importing a range of products: hand-painted objects, glassware, and pottery. I added a line of overtly Christian items like crucifixes, mosaic plaques, holy water, Biblical puzzles, and my most popular item, a videotape about the life of Jesus.

I did some market research but not nearly enough—and the research I did was not of high quality. I had sold myself on the concept, and I wanted so badly for it to succeed that I ignored all signs that it might not.

I did bring some of my products to a few churches in Berkeley to gauge the response, but I didn't pay much attention to the lukewarm reaction they received. I was simply convinced that my concept would work. Besides, the local Berkeley churches weren't my target audience; the real customers would be a different strain of Christian in Dallas or Houston or the small towns of the south.

I hired a Christian marketing consultant, as well as another consultant with expertise in catalog sales.

I understood, very clearly, the irony of a Jewish guy selling crucifixes, so in my marketing I was careful to fit into the born-again Christian world. Aware that a Berkeley, California, address might raise eyebrows in the Bible Belt, I rented a post office box in El Cerrito. It sounded like the name of a suburb in conservative Orange County, but in fact El Cerrito is just north of Berkeley. Instead of using my real name in catalogs and correspondence, I used a pseudonym, Norman Charles.

I was warehousing the products in an old Quonset hut adjacent to the Berkeley Jewish Community Center and had my nephew Mike helping me out. At moments, it felt absurd, these two Jewish guys knee deep in cartons of crucifixes and Jesus videos.

"Mike," I'd say, "can you grab me a case of holy water?"

"Coming right up."

Occasionally we found ourselves looking at each other, as if to say, what are we doing here?

At the same time, I was gradually delving into my own religion, with the help of Yehuda Ferris, the rabbi of the local Chabad house. So I asked Rabbi Ferris his opinion of what I was doing with Gifts from the Holy Land. As usual, he was consistent and thoughtful. He didn't take issue with my business on religious grounds, he said, but he had one question: "Is this really what you want to be doing?"

That gave me pause. I didn't have a good response. If I had been honest with myself, I would have acknowledged that I was uncomfortable with the business. Some of that discomfort led to the three major mistakes I made with Gifts from the Holy Land:

I didn't know my customers.

I didn't invest as much money as would have
    been required to succeed.

I let my emotions cloud my business judgment.

It's vital in any business to know as much as possible about your customers. You need to know what they eat for breakfast and what they do all day. The more you know about your customers, the better you can serve their needs and, in turn, the more the business will thrive.

I simply didn't know my customers as well as I should have. I didn't bother to make trips to South Carolina or Texas to market my Holy Land products because deep down, I simply didn't want to. I was passionate about the idea but not about developing close ties with my customers.

As a result of my hands-off approach, I missed the mark. I was trying to sell to Christians as a whole without understanding something basic: that different denominations had very different needs. What appealed to one might offend another. I didn't know that Mormons don't use crosses or that holy water holds no appeal for anybody but Catholics. I didn't bother to research, to assess the demand, and to attune myself to my customers' varied needs and perspectives.

That was a superb lesson in how *not* to run a business.

To make matters worse, I failed to invest financially in Gifts from the Holy Land at the level the business required. My consultant told me that venturing into the mail-order business was a million-dollar proposition. I didn't believe it. I convinced myself that I knew more than the consultant. Confidence is a positive trait, but hubris rarely works.

Sometimes it's important to listen to your *shtetl*-mates.

What I learned is that running a mail-order business is like fishing. You throw out a few lines and you reel them in. You reel in nothing once, twice, three times. Then you get a nibble, so you throw more lines in that direction. Catalog marketing required a huge investment and extensive experimentation. You have to spend a lot of money on postage and printing before you start seeing sales. (The return can be huge: even now, with the domination of the Internet, certain catalogs still sell much more than many Web sites.)

The biggest problem with Gifts from the Holy Land was that I let my excitement cloud my judgment. It was my older brother Fred, an astute businessperson, who pointed this out to me in stark terms. "Are you running a crusade," he asked, "or a business?" Having enthusiasm for an enterprise is essential, but when your passion blinds you to good business planning, you're sunk.

When the low level of business slowed to a mere trickle, I came to realize that I needed to shut down. I liquidated the inventory, leaving it on consignment at some Christian stores. Finally it was down to just the last few cases of holy water. I couldn't just pour them down the drain. I took them to one Christian store, walked in, and just said, "Where do you want the holy water?" Before the person I spoke to even answered, I put down the four cases and bolted out the door.

~

That was my first failure, and it was devastating. I lost about fifty thousand dollars. It wasn't a giant amount of money in start-up business terms, but the psychological defeat was painful.

I was a lifelong competitor. Even my childhood summer camp was all about winning. Everything counted: "Race you to the tree! I won!"

Now I had lost. I was out of work.

It felt awful at the time, but with perspective I have come to understand that the failure of Gifts from the Holy Land was a blessing—just one more step toward the ventures I was really meant to run. I learned lessons that continue to serve me—not just about market research and customer service, but about how important it is to create companies that truly resonate with your soul. It made me hungrier and more eager than ever to succeed.

Perhaps most importantly, I learned that I could fail and survive. Like the generations of Jews, each certain it might be the last, I rebounded and used adversity and disappointment to adapt and grow, staying ever truer to myself.

One who wants to enter the holiness of the day must first lay down the profanity of clattering commerce, of being yoked to toil. . . . He must say farewell to manual work and learn to understand that the world has already been created and will survive without the help of man.

—ABRAHAM JOSHUA HESCHEL, *THE SABBATH*

CHAPTER SEVEN

Remember the Sabbath

There's an old Jewish story about a pianist who was asked how he was able to play the notes so beautifully.

"The notes I handle no better than many pianists," he answered, "but the pauses between the notes—ah, that is where the art resides."

The same is true in life and in business. We live in a world that has become increasingly focused on working ceaselessly. It seems that every device touted as making our lives easier and freeing up time does just the opposite. Today, people constantly check their e-mail in bed, send text messages while they drive, pull out their laptops over dinner, and answer business calls at their kids' soccer games. These people aren't working less. They're working *constantly*. They need to listen to the words of the pianist: Forget about playing the notes. Focus on the pauses.

What's a chapter about pause and rest doing in a book about business? This isn't a book only about work. It's about how to be an entrepreneur while still living a healthy, meaningful, worthwhile life. The Jewish tradition says you cannot do that without the Sabbath—without building into your life some form of pause, of stepping away from the work. Shabbat is perhaps the Jewish people's single most significant contribution to humanity. I have heard it called the original weekend.

To me, Shabbat is not only about rest but also about renewal. It's an opportunity to "recharge the batteries"— the essential pause that provides energy for the rest of the week.

If you're not Jewish—and even if you are—you don't have to observe the Sabbath by taking twenty-five hours a week off or by doing so in keeping with the traditional manner of observance. You should, however, build significant pauses into your life. You'll find yourself more creative and more productive—not to mention happier.

I have heard this message over the years, sometimes from unlikely messengers.

After the sale of Noah's Bagels, I agreed to stay on for a year as a consultant with the new company. My responsibilities were sparse and somewhat symbolic: attending monthly board meetings, visiting far-flung stores, and showing up for ceremonial occasions. That year I did face one crisis—just as the Einstein/Noah Bagel Corp. board was preparing to take the company public, a routine, voluntary inspection turned up a slightly elevated level of the bacteria listeria in the lox in one of the stores. Listeria is common and expected in smoked fish, and I learned that the very slightly higher level detected posed only an extremely remote potential danger. However, since listeria can be fatal, we jumped on fixing the problem, immediately removing the fish from the stores so that the danger decreased substantially. However, the new CEO was concerned that the information might become public. Out of an abundance of caution he opted to take the offensive, issuing a low-key statement explaining that we were pulling the product in question from the stores.

He also brought in a media trainer who specialized in corporate damage control to prepare our team just in case the situation became serious. As I was then vice-chairman of the parent company and mine was still the name over the door, I was given the job of handling the press in a worst-case scenario: if a customer died from the bacteria. The trainer videotaped me practicing answers to hypothetical questions. I was very uncomfortable as I watched the tape and thought I looked like a bumbling idiot. The trainer taught me the importance of sound bites, training me to talk like a politician with a few stock answers: "Our heart goes out to the family." "We mourn their loss." "No words can adequately express how I feel."

Even though it was completely hypothetical, I found the whole experience to be incredibly stressful, and I told the media trainer I didn't envy him his work, traveling the country to intervene in crises. "What a job!" I said to him. "You fly in when all hell is breaking loose, and then you have to work quickly to get these stressed-out executives on message."

He nodded and smiled. "The only way I survive," he said, "is Shabbat."

I was astounded. He wasn't wearing a yarmulke, and I hadn't even realized that the man was Jewish. His answer made perfect sense. I had experienced the same feeling over the years. No matter how difficult my week, no matter how long the hours, no matter how frustrating the conflicts I encountered, I could handle them—in part because I knew that I would have a day to step back from it all, to enjoy life, to pay attention to matters that were much more important than inventories, business plans, and payrolls.

In the words of the great theologian Abraham Joshua Heschel (in *Between God and Man*), "It is one thing to race or be driven by the vicissitudes that menace life, and another thing to stand still and to embrace the presence of an eternal moment."

The Essential Need for Rest

It's hard to embrace the presence of an eternal moment when you're knee-deep in the mundane details of running a business. I didn't always fully embrace Shabbat; I came to full observance of it only recently. Looking back, though, I certainly needed it. As early as my midtwenties, when I was running Bread & Circus, I had the feeling of imprisonment that can come with running a small retail operation. When you're the proprietor, you're the one who is responsible for minding every detail. Especially in the early days of a business, it can feel like being in a cage. Either you're there minding the store or you're worried about the person who is minding the store—or you're panicked that nobody is minding the store.

Perhaps it's in response to that overwhelming burden that I have punctuated my life with informal, self-imposed sabbaticals. The sabbatical itself is a concept that stems from the Torah, which called for a seven-year agricultural cycle in which the Israelites were to cease all agricultural activity (planting, plowing, and harvesting) in the *shmita*, or seventh year, and let the land lie fallow. (In addition, at the year's end, all debts are nullified.) In modern-day Israel, many observant Jews still abide by the *shmita* cycle.

Just as Biblical sabbaticals would provide a break from routine and allow the land to regenerate, my own sabbaticals have been times of personal renewal. I sometimes feel as if I have only two buttons: one says "Off"; the other says "On." I don't have an in-between speed. When I'm working, I go full speed ahead. When I'm off, though, I shut off the world of work and take pleasure in the rest and relaxation and diversion.

That's what I did after I sold Bread & Circus at the age of twenty-nine and I traveled through Europe. For three months I made my way from place to place on a Eurailpass, exploring the continent for the first time, drinking up the sights and smells and the different cultures I encountered almost daily, and savoring the thrill of feeling free.

After I sold Alper International, I took my first trip to Israel, which provided me with another opportunity to step away from the routine and see my life and career in a fresh perspective. Of course, that visit also helped to spark my interest in Judaism. Without that rest, I might never have founded Noah's Bagels.

Traditional Shabbat

For a long time I was resistant to what I perceived as the strictures of Shabbat. Traditionally, Jews mark Shabbat by emulating what God did at the end of the Biblical narrative of Genesis. After toiling for six days to create the world, God rested on the seventh day. Similarly, Shabbat marks a moment of pause, of refraining from the work of creation in which we engage all week. Rabbinic sources came to define work as any of thirty-nine *melachot*, categories of activities that were required in the building of the ancient tabernacle—actions like plowing, grinding, baking, and burning. Essentially, they are all activities in which humans exert control over their environment. Over the centuries, rabbis have interpreted and reinterpreted the laws of Shabbat to forbid activities like lighting a stove, working in the garden, or writing on a computer. (Just as with any practice, there is a full spectrum of observance, ranging from lenient to strict.)

From my youngest days, I have resisted rules, so even though I felt myself drawn to the idea of traditional Jewish observance and I loved the *idea* of Shabbat, I steered clear of the more strict observances. It didn't sound peaceful to me. It sounded like a lot of limits. I wanted my freedom.

Then one Saturday morning I noticed a fellow in a yarmulke and a suit walking through my Berkeley neighborhood. Talk about alternative lifestyles! It's rare to see a man in a suit in laid-back, liberal Berkeley at any time, let alone on a lazy Saturday morning—and with a yarmulke! I started chatting with him and learned that he was walking to synagogue. The next week I joined Eric. It was a fifty-five-minute walk to the nearest Modern Orthodox synagogue. It was a lovely stroll, and the two-and-a-half-hour service, all in Hebrew, felt warm and welcoming, albeit somewhat difficult to sit through. I went back the next week. After a while, it became my routine to walk to *shul* with Eric on Shabbat mornings, often stopping for a traditional Shabbat lunch at his home.

Over time, I came to think of the rules and restrictions as gifts, ways of offering freedom from the chores and routines of the week. Acting differently made Shabbat feel special—more like what Heschel has described as a "palace in time."

When I opened Noah's Bagels, I was not yet fully observant, but Hope and I had certainly made Shabbat part of our lives. We gathered the family for a relaxing and sumptuous Friday night dinner with the traditional challah and Jewish favorites such as herring in wine sauce, matzah ball soup, chicken, noodle kugel, and a fine kosher Merlot. We set aside time to spend with each other, and I took the day away from work.

That was a difficult trick to pull off in the early days of the business, when it seemed that everything required my personal attention and my instinct was to keep a tight rein on the operation. As it turned out, obtaining kosher certification wasn't just a matter of checking ingredients and steering clear of forbidden items such as shellfish and pork. In many communities, the rabbis also require that kosher restaurants be closed on Shabbat.

I knew that a bagel shop couldn't survive in Berkeley, California, without doing business on Saturday mornings—one of the busiest times of the week. It was a formula for failure. So I worked out an arrangement the rabbis called in Hebrew a *shtar mechira*, a legal provision by which I technically sold the store to a non-Jew for one day a week (plus many Jewish holidays observed similarly to Shabbat) for a nominal sum and then at the end of the day purchased it back for the same sum. It seemed like legal fiction, but in fact it was testimony to both the integrity and flexibility of halacha, Jewish law. Since there were so few kosher eateries in the Bay Area, the rabbis saw the benefit to the community as so important that the law could bend a bit. (Once again, Jews were finding new ways to keep their culture intact by being flexible.)

Though the law could bend, it was difficult for me to step away and let somebody else run the business. I had to honor the *shtar mechira*, the legal agreement, so I completely refrained from involvement with the business from sundown on Friday until the stars came out on Saturday night. I told my employees not even to phone me, no matter what came up.

Of course, that meant I had to find a manager I could trust. Whenever you open a retail operation, you have what is sometimes called a break-in crew—that is, the initial team that likely won't last. The work can be difficult, but they are the people you need to get the operation off the ground. I hired a manager named Happy Shaughnessy, a man who lived up to his name: bright red cheeks, always smiling and upbeat. Happy had worked as a bartender on the Mardi Gras parade route in New Orleans and loved it. I figured that anyone who could love that work would be great managing my weekend throngs. So he was my first manager and the first signer of the *shtar mechira*. I turned over the restaurant to him—literally— every Friday afternoon.

I would head home, challah under my arm (we baked our own delicious egg challah, based on a recipe from a local Oakland baker), content in the knowledge that I would not have to worry about the bagel business for a day. That break each week is probably what kept me sane and functional while the business grew. On many days I would be called in very early in the morning to taste-test lox or herring or tend to some disaster while it was still dark outside and I was barely awake. Not on Shabbat.

Some entrepreneurs might find it difficult to fathom stepping away from business even for a day, but the more I did it, the easier—and more essential—it became. Knowing I could leave for a day reassured me that I didn't have to worry when significant Jewish holidays came around. Less than two months after Noah's first opened its doors, Hope and I took our sons on a retreat for Rosh Hashanah, joining other families in the Santa Cruz Mountains to mark the Jewish New Year. Even in the midst of the intense craziness of launching a new retail operation, with all of its attendant details, I stepped away and focused on matters far more eternal.

Noah's took another significant break each year for a Jewish holiday, closing for the eight days of Passover. On Passover, Jews refrain from eating leavened bread to commemorate the matzah the ancient Israelites ate as they fled Egypt. It's forbidden even to *own* leavened products during the holiday. I didn't need to close the store for Passover; the same Jewish legal arrangement that allowed the store to be open on Saturdays would have allowed for Passover as well. To me, though, it was essential to the store's Jewish identity and mission to close for that period—even at significant financial peril. I felt it was vital to the integrity of the enterprise, to keeping it a Jewish business.

The reactions were fascinating. Many of our Christian customers expressed understanding and even admiration for our decision and the spiritual message it sent. It was the nonobservant Jewish customers who were bent out of shape. One wholesale client, the owner of Zack's Deli, was so angry to lose the week's supply of "bagel shticks" (long, straight bagel rolls) his customers loved that he threatened to stop buying from me altogether if I didn't make sure he got them. I took a guess that the original Zack had been his father and said, "Zack would not have done that."

That made him pause, but he still insisted on dropping us. Then, two days after Passover, he called somewhat sheepishly to ask for his bagel shticks back. (He couldn't find better ones elsewhere.)

While such observances were important to me when I ran the bagel business, it was only after the sale of Noah's, when my family spent the year in Jerusalem, that I became fully observant of Shabbat. Jerusalem can have that affect on a person. That autumn we rented an apartment in the Greek Colony, a lovely leafy neighborhood not far from a fashionable street with all the necessary neighborhood amenities: a bank, a green grocer, many cafes and restaurants. During the week it was bustling. On Shabbat all of that stopped.

In the Middle East, everything feels intense and extreme: the weather, the emotions, the relationships, the food. Never did I feel that more than in the transition from the weekday to Shabbat. In the hours before sundown, as shopkeepers begin pulling down their shutters and locking the doors, traffic slows and busses finish their rounds. The smells of roast chicken and brisket permeate the air, and men can be seen dashing home, carrying bouquets for the Shabbat table. Then, precisely at the appointed minute, a siren sounds—a wailing blast that can be heard throughout the city—and a peaceful silence takes hold. After that, the people are all on foot, walking purposefully to synagogue for evening services.

I found it intoxicating: the tranquility, the singing of ancient tunes reverberating against the stone walls of the synagogue, the Thanksgiving-style meals in every home. My time in Jerusalem gave me a taste of traditional Shabbat as something normal—everybody was on the same page. I was not the out-of-sync one, the lone observant one. I felt grounded, centered, and content. Just as my first trip to Israel had given me a sense of suddenly feeling at home, being part of this community made me feel at home in my religion.

My wife, Hope, came to this lifestyle more gradually. She knew that when I become passionate about something, I tend to embrace it with fervor, so she worried that I was going to become *haredi* (the Hebrew term for "ultraorthodox"), spending my Saturdays hanging out with men in black hats and long beards. In truth, I have never been extremist in my religious practice. Everything I have ever taken on has happened slowly, over years, even decades. In time, my wife supported me in my Shabbat observance.

When we returned from Jerusalem to Berkeley, I had a new confidence and the feeling of being grounded in tradition. I had come too far to turn back and now fully embraced a Shabbat-observant lifestyle. Of course I am the same person—the same rebel at heart. At my core, I still resist the idea of rules imposed on me, but I also embrace a lifestyle that can bring to our Berkeley home a feeling of peace, serenity, and community similar to what I experienced in Jerusalem.

I do not wear the rules of Shabbat like a tight corset. I see these laws as guidelines, structures meant not to serve as chores but to enhance the joy of the day.

Traditionally, Jews are forbidden from even discussing business on Shabbat. Talk of money is out of the question. In some circles, if you find yourself mentioning U.S. currency, you use the term *doll hairs*, with a wink and a nod to acknowledge that this really isn't "Shabbes talk." Technically, the halacha doesn't allow using the time on Shabbat to make plans for events that will happen after Shabbat. The purpose is not to deny pleasure but to relax the mind and the heart, to give one the chance to focus on the moment rather than worrying about what has passed or what is yet to come.

For all the emphasis on spiritual rest, perhaps the most transformative Shabbat rest for me is physical. Every Shabbat afternoon I take a *Shabbes shluf*, my sacred snooze. It's the only day I nap, but I can't live without that nap, and it magically brings rest into my entire week. That was a custom I started while I was running Noah's, and somehow I could get through even the most hectic, crazy weeks of work, knowing that at week's end, I could grab those couple hours of *menucha* (Hebrew for "rest").

Bringing Rest into Your Life

I could not have written this book about business without including a section on Shabbat. It has been so important to my life and success that I cannot imagine my life without it. The point, though, isn't that every entrepreneur needs Shabbat per se. It's that you need to build pauses—in months, days, or even minutes—into your life and into your business.

That's even more important these days, when work can permeate every moment of your day. Nothing drives me crazier than being at a movie or in a nice restaurant and hearing people jabbering away on their cell phones. It's essential to find ways to stop, to cut off the noise and clatter of life, and to experience calm and clarity. In our home, we have a rule against taking or making any phone calls during dinner—a small step toward blocking out the distractions of the world.

I tend to be quite manic, throwing myself into my work, buzzing around all day, bursting with ideas, plans, questions, and schemes. Then, at times, I need to just pause.

Cutting all of that off is not just shutting down; it's a way of asserting power, of controlling one's life.

It's a simple reality that many entrepreneurs fail to grasp: Often, the best way to serve your business is to step away from it. Working nonstop does not solve problems, nor does it make you a better businessperson. It is guaranteed to produce burnout, boredom, and fatigue. It robs you of the opportunity to gain perspective on your work and life.

When I work with entrepreneurs, one of my first pieces of advice is to step away, to take a working vacation. If a client were to run a hotdog stand, I'd suggest taking a week every year to travel around the country visiting hotdog stands, seeing what works elsewhere, what doesn't work, what unique practice is worth bringing home. It's a working vacation but one that can help to transform you and your business. Just running on the same daily treadmill of work doesn't serve anybody. It leaves no room for growth, expansion, or imagination.

The same is true for boosting morale and building strong teams in the workplace. When I hire new employees to important positions, I like to do something unusual and enjoyable with them: take a hike, go for a swim, head out for a bike ride. Playing golf can accomplish the same goal. It's an opportunity to start the relationship with a solid foundation and to send the message that I take them seriously not just as a worker but as a person. Management retreats, too, are vital chances to build the kind of strong relationships that help businesses thrive and make people feel more invested in the enterprise.

~

It's vital to get away from the day-to-day routine and take time to envision what your business and your career might be. If you don't allow yourself to do that, not only are your chances for expansion and growth limited, but your core business will likely suffer as well. Many people think they can't afford to take the time to get away. I would argue that you can't afford *not* to go.

Even small efforts pay off. When Noah's Bagels was in the midst of its rapid growth, I would routinely leave the office for a solitary forty-five–minute walk without a cell phone. The fresh air and the break in routine helped clear my head, and it often became the time when the best ideas came to me.

I sometimes hear people going on about years without a vacation, so dedicated are they to their work. This never impresses me. Successful people understand that downtime is just as important as time on the job. Vacations have always been an important part of my life.

When you're running a business, it's easy to feel like you're indispensable. That's what your ego wants you to think. I advocate doing the opposite: step away, get perspective, and then return refreshed and renewed.

It is not up to you to complete the work,
yet you are not free to desist from it.

—RABBI TARPHON, PIRKEI AVOT

The Eighth Day

Shabbat doesn't last forever, nor should it. The purpose of stepping away from work—whether for a month, a day, or an hour—is not simply to rest. It is to recharge your batteries, to renew the body, soul, and mind and return to the world refreshed and even changed.

While the seven-day cycle is a preeminent theme in Judaism, the eighth day has a power of its own. God created the world in six days and then rested on the seventh day. On the eighth day, it is the job of human beings to pick up where God left off and to start the work of perfecting the world. Judaism has a term for that task: *tikkun olam*, the process of repairing the world.

American society places a premium on leisure for its own sake. Whole industries spring up around spas, beach resorts, luxury cruises, and doing nothing. Generations of Americans have also come to focus on retirement, spending decades planning for the day when you can stop working and simply relax.

The truth is that retirement is not the ideal it's cracked up to be. You can only do nothing for so long. Then it gets boring. In fact, statistics show a correlation between retirement and early death. At the dawn of my career as an entrepreneur, a wise old man—the foreman of the Vermont factory where I bought the wooden bowls—gave me a piece of advice: "A man needs a place to go in the morning." (The same could apply to a woman, of course.) An ancient Jewish text, Avot d'Rabbi Natan, carries a similar message from a rabbi named Yosi: "A man can die if he has nothing to do."

Retirement has evolved to reflect that need and desire. Whether you are out of work by design or it has been forced on you because of corporate downsizing, job elimination, or the troubled economy, it's important to have a purpose every day. That's another essential message of Judaism: when your work is complete, it's not time to retreat from the world entirely; its time to use your skills, talents, and passions to contribute to the world, to reach out and fix what you can.

Of course, it's also time to reflect and assess. When I look back on my own life, I see that as much as I have tried to live with purpose and direction, sometimes I am struck by a perennial Jewish question: Do we guide our own lives, or are we guided by some higher power? Do we choose our own fate, or is it chosen for us?

One of the most thrilling days of my career came in 1993 when Noah's Bagels received a telephone call from someone claiming to be a staffer at the White House. At first I didn't believe it, but I returned the call to a number in Washington, D.C., and it was indeed true. President Clinton would be visiting the Bay Area and staying at a hotel in Oakland. The staffer asked that we deliver bagels for his breakfast.

Early on the appointed morning, I made the delivery in person. The White House staff had ordered many dozens of bagels, and I oversaw the production to make sure they were top quality. I put on a white baker's outfit, complete with a shirt with my name on it, and drove to the hotel. When I arrived, the security people would not let me up to the president's suite, so I handed over the boxes of bagels to a Secret Service officer.

Waiting for my audience with the president, I joined a throng of reporters and others waiting behind a cordon. I approached Wolf Blitzer from CNN and introduced myself, telling him I had brought bagels for the president. I thought perhaps he would take out his microphone and interview me.

"So, where are they?" he said.

"Who?"

"Where are the bagels?"

It was eight o'clock in the morning and the press corps was hungry.

As I waited, it became clear to me that I was not going to meet the president. At most, I might catch a glimpse of him. Finally, his limousine appeared, and as I stood at attention with the kitchen staff and the reporters, suddenly I caught sight of the limousine and, through the window, President Clinton.

At that moment, I had what I can only describe as a religious vision. I immediately flashed on the Biblical story of Joseph, who, in prison in Egypt, interprets the dreams of the pharaoh's baker. In the dream the baker was carrying three baskets of baked goods on his head for the pharaoh, when birds came and ate the food. Joseph tells him the interpretation, which ultimately proves true: in three days the pharaoh will have the baker beheaded.

As I stood there in my white baker's outfit, I realized that like the Biblical baker, on that day, I had been the baker for the most powerful man in the world. But as high as I felt, I realized that it could all be taken away. I could bask in the fame for a few hours or days, but soon it could be gone.

That stark realization reinforced what I have always believed: What is important is not your status, the profit you make from one transaction, your salary, or your company's annual sales. What's important is providing for your family, conducting yourself with integrity, and living a life of meaning.

Glossary of Jewish Terms

ba'al teshuva   Literally "master of return," a Jew who has newly embraced traditional Jewish practice.

bashert   Destined; fated; meant to be (Yiddish).

Chabad   One of the largest Hassidic movements of Orthodox Judaism, with thousands of outreach centers around the world. Also known as Lubavich. The Hebrew "ch" sound, which doesn't exist in English, is pronounced as in the name of the composer Bach.

challah   (Also spelled *hallah*) Braided bread eaten at Shabbat meals.

chutzpah   Nerve combined with a dash of arrogance.

dan l'chaf zechut   Hebrew expression meaning "to give someone the benefit of the doubt."

hakn shisl   A wooden chopping bowl (Yiddish).

halacha   Literally "the way," the term for the body of Jewish law.

haredi   Hebrew for "ultraorthodox."

hora   The most popular Israeli folk dance, a staple of Jewish weddings.

kashrut   See **kosher.**

kosher   Literally "fit"; acceptable according to Jewish dietary law, known as kashrut. The most significant laws of kashrut forbid consuming milk and dairy products together and prohibit the eating pork and shellfish entirely.

lech lecha   Hebrew for "go forth" or "go to yourself." God's first command to Abraham in the Bible (Genesis 12:1).

matzah   Unleavened bread eaten during the holiday of Passover in commemoration of the bread that didn't have time to rise as the Biblical Israelites fled Egypt.

melachot   The thirty-nine categories of creative activities that traditional Jewish law forbids on the Sabbath.

mensch   Yiddish for "human being," often used to mean a decent, upstanding person.

menschlichkeit   Humanity, the quality of being a mensch.

menucha   Hebrew for "rest."

meshuga le'davar   Hebrew phrase meaning "crazy for the thing"; obsessively, single-mindedly devoted to a cause or project.

mezuzah   A piece of parchment (usually in a decorative case) inscribed with certain verses from the Torah and placed on the doorframe of a Jewish home or establishment.

Mishna   The collection of oral laws compiled about 200 CE by Rabbi Judah ha-Nasi and forming the basic part of the Talmud.

na'aseh v'nishma   Hebrew Biblical phrase (Exodus 24:7) literally meaning "we will do and we will hear (or understand)." Biblical commentators understand it as the basis for the Jewish emphasis on action over mere contemplation as the root of faith.

pareve   In kashrut, containing neither meat nor dairy ingredients; neutral.

pas Yisroel   Literally "bread of an Israelite," a strict kashrut designation requiring that a Jew be involved in the baking process.

Passover (Hebrew: Pesach) The eight-day spring festival commemorating the ancient Israelites' exodus from Egypt. Traditionally, Jews do not eat bread or any leavened products during Passover.

Pirke Avot Known as Ethics of the Fathers, a section of the Mishna containing ethical teachings.

pushke A small container in which money for *tzedaka* is collected.

rebbe Yiddish for "rabbi" or "teacher," often referring to a person in the role of guru or mentor.

Shabbat; Shabbes The Jewish Sabbath, lasting from sundown Friday until nightfall Saturday. The Sephardic pronunciation—widely used in Israel and elsewhere—is "Shah-BOT," while the Ashkenazic pronunciation of the same Hebrew word is "SHAH-biss."

shalom Hebrew for "peace," used as goodbye and hello.

shidduch Yiddish for "a match," usually referring to a connection made by a matchmaker between a potential husband and wife, but often used to refer to a union of any two people or institutions.

shluf Yiddish for "nap."

shmear Yiddish for "spread," as in "Give me a *shmear* of cream cheese."

shmita Also known as the sabbatical year, the seventh year of the seven-year agricultural cycle mandated by the Torah.

shpilkes Yiddish for "pins." To "have shpilkes" is to be in a state of nervous agitation.

shtar mechira A legal provision by which a Jewish owner transfers a business temporarily to a non-Jewish owner for the duration of Shabbat or a holiday, thereby enabling a kosher establishment to remain open on those days without violating Jewish law.

shtetl   A small Jewish village or town in Eastern Europe, such as the one depicted in *Fiddler on the Roof*.

shul   Yiddish for "synagogue."

tachlis   Yiddish for "point" or "purpose," used to mean "brass tacks."

tikkun olam   Hebrew for "repairing the world" or "healing the world," a central tenet of Judaism, stating that one is obligated to work for the betterment of the world.

treif   Not kosher. The literal Hebrew meaning is "torn," as meat torn from a live animal is not kosher.

tsotskies   Yiddish for "knickknacks" or "bric-a-brac."

tzedaka   Hebrew for "justice," often used to mean "charity."

yarmulke   Yiddish word for the skullcap traditionally worn by Jewish men. In Hebrew it is called a *kippa*.

yeshiva   A religious seminary where Torah, Talmud, and other traditional Jewish texts are studied.

yetzer hara   Hebrew for evil inclination.

Acknowledgments

I thank my coauthor, Tom Fields-Meyer, who was able to synthesize my work into an organized and smooth narrative. His greatest contribution was his ability to distill a life's worth of experience into a compelling story. He was truly a pleasure to work with.

I am also indebted to Miriam Petruck of the Perfect Word for her timely and well-researched suggestions and to Lisa Klug, who was very helpful in sharing the details of her own book writing experience. Rabbi Yehuda Ferris and Rabbi Yonatan Cohen not only fielded inquiries of a spiritual nature but were also very helpful in making editorial suggestions that made religious thought come to life.

Richard Pechner was extremely helpful in the process of categorizing, selecting, and preserving archival photos. Jesse Buckner-Alper was extraordinary in expediting prepublication materials.

I am also grateful for important encouragement, suggestions, editorial assistance, and comments from Joel Ackerman, Spike Alper, Alice Buckner, Julie Doughty, Shawn Fields-Meyer, Dan Fingerman, Paul Hamburg, Nancy Hauge, Murray Kalis, Andrea Michaels, Daniel Perlman, Harry Pollack, William Rosenzweig, Michael Shulman, Andrea Siegel, and Judith Smith.

It certainly took a shtetl to write this book, but in particular, I would like to thank my wife, Hope, who was patient beyond belief regarding the smallest details as well as the largest global questions. The book would not have been possible without her. Hope's vision and practical suggestions were invaluable—not to mention her willingness to put up with me during this process.

To my sons Jesse, David, and Robbie—always my greatest fans. I thank them for their patience with my many foibles.

Finally I thank my father, David E. Alper *z"l* (of blessed memory), whose business instincts were second to none and whose ideals and values are with me constantly.

About the Author

Less than seven years after Noah Alper founded Noah's Bagels, the popular West Coast company sold for one hundred million dollars, highlighting four decades of entrepreneurship that have given Alper, now a consultant, a well of wisdom about creating and growing businesses while staying true to core values. He is also the founder of the natural-food chain Bread & Circus, once the Northeast's largest natural grocery store and now owned by Whole Foods Market. He lives in Berkeley, California, with his wife, Hope, and is the father of three sons, Jesse, David, and Robbie.